FINAL SALUTE

ALSO BY JIM SHEELER

Obit:

Inspiring Stories of Ordinary People
Who Led Extraordinary Lives

FINAL SALUTE

A Story of Unfinished Lives

Jim Sheeler

THE PENGUIN PRESS

NEW YORK

2008

THE PENGUIN PRESS
Published by the Penguin Group
Penguin Group (USA) Inc., 375 Hudson Street, New York, New York 10014, U.S.A. ·
Penguin Group (Canada), 90 Eglinton Avenue East, Suite 700, Toronto, Ontario,
Canada M4P 2Y3 (a division of Pearson Penguin Canada Inc.) · Penguin Books Ltd,
80 Strand, London WC2R ORL, England · Penguin Ireland, 25 St Stephen's Green,
Dublin 2, Ireland (a division of Penguin Books Ltd) · Penguin Books Australia Ltd,
250 Camberwell Road, Camberwell, Victoria 3124, Australia (a division of Pearson Australia
Group Pty Ltd) · Penguin Books India Pvt Ltd, 11 Community Centre, Panchsheel Park,
New Delhi – 110 017, India · Penguin Group (NZ), 67 Apollo Drive, Rosedale, North Shore
0632, New Zealand (a division of Pearson New Zealand Ltd) · Penguin Books (South
Africa) (Pty) Ltd, 24 Sturdee Avenue, Rosebank, Johannesburg 2196, South Africa

Penguin Books Ltd, Registered Offices:
80 Strand, London WC2R 0RL, England

First published in 2008 by The Penguin Press,
a member of Penguin Group (USA) Inc.

Copyright © Jim Sheeler, 2008
All rights reserved

Portions of this book first appeared as a series of articles in the
Rocky Mountain News. Copyright © 2003, 2004, 2005, 2006, 2007
by Denver Publishing Company.

Photographs reproduced by permission of the *Rocky Mountain News.*

"Warrior's Tribute" lyrics by Wil Numkena. Copyright © 2003 Firedrum Music ASCAP,
www.soundofamerica.com, reprinted courtesy of The Soar Corporation.

Library of Congress Cataloging-in-Publication Data
Sheeler, Jim.
Final salute : a story of unfinished lives / by Jim Sheeler.
p. cm.
ISBN 978-1-59420-165-3
1. Death notification—United States. 2. Military ceremonies, honors,
and salutes—United States. 3. Iraq war, 2003—Casualties. 4. Death—Psychological
aspects. 5. Bereavement—Psychological aspects. 6. Families of military
personnel—United States. I. Title.
U353.S53 2008
956.7044'37—dc22   2007044130

Printed in the United States of America
1 3 5 7 9 10 8 6 4 2

DESIGNED BY STEPHANIE HUNTWORK

For everyone who opened the door

CONTENTS

PART I

THE KNOCK

You can almost see the blood run out of their body and their
heart hit the floor. It's not the blood as much as their soul.
Something sinks. I've never seen that except when
someone dies. And I've seen a lot of death.

— MAJOR STEVE BECK

Marine Lance Corporal
Kyle W. Burns

Laramie, Wyoming

THERE WERE NO footprints in the snow.

The thought struck the Marine major as he stared from his truck at the pristine white powder on the sidewalk of the dark neighborhood street in Wyoming. Soft flakes struck the warm windshield, then melted and dripped down the glass.

Every second the major waited was one more tick of his wristwatch that, for the family inside the house, everything remained the same. To the major, the small wooden home looked as if it could have been dropped from his own hometown in Oklahoma—a house his own mother might have lived in if she were still alive. Now he had to walk up to someone else's mother, carrying the name of someone else's son.

Less than an hour earlier, just outside Laramie, the major and his passenger, a gunnery sergeant, pulled the Chevy Suburban into a small gas station and grabbed their garment bags.

The two men walked into the station dressed in street clothes. When they emerged from the restroom, their spit-shined black shoes clicked on the floor. Their dark blue pants, lined with a red stripe signifying past bloodshed, fell straight. Their dress blue jackets wrapped their necks with a high collar that dates back to the Revolutionary War when Marines wore leather neckstraps to protect them from enemy swords. As they walked out of the gas station, the major felt the eyes of the clerk.

He knows, the major thought.

Once they arrived at the wooden home blanketed in snow, the major looked at his watch. When he had left Denver hours earlier, it was still November 11, Veterans Day, named for the eleventh hour of the eleventh month of the eleventh day of 1918 when an armistice declared an end to "the war to end all wars."

In Wyoming, it was well past midnight. Veterans Day was over.

Throughout the two-hour drive, the major imagined what would happen at the door and what he would say once it opened. This was his second notification. He had easily memorized the words in the acronym-studded manual:

Although no firm instructions can be given to cover the varied and sometimes difficult situations that may arise when making personal notifications, the following guidance applies:

1. The visit may last as long as necessary; however, remain cognizant of the next of kin (NOK)'s right to privacy and do not remain longer than necessary.

2. Before beginning notification, verbally verify that the correct person is being addressed.

3. If the NOK does not offer entrance into the home, ask permission to enter. It is helpful if the NOK is seated prior to delivering the news.

4. Use good judgment and do not pass gory or embarrassing details.

5. When addressing the casualty's family, make every effort to display an understanding and helpful demeanor which will give comfort to a bereaved family.

6. Speak naturally and at a normal pace. An overly formal approach or a flippant manner may seriously damage the Marine Corps' reputation with the family, and possibly an entire community. The following is suggested and may be modified as appropriate:

DEATH CASES: "The Commandant of the Marine Corps has entrusted me to express his deep regret that your (relationship), John, (died/was killed in action) in (place of incident) (city/state or country) on (date). (State the circumstances.) The Commandant extends his deepest sympathy to you and your family in your loss."

The major never liked scripts.

. . .

E VERY DOOR IS different. Some are ornately hand-carved hardwood; some are hollow tin. Some are protected by elaborate security systems, some by flapping screens. The doors are all that stand between a family and the message.

For Major Steve Beck it starts with a knock or a ring of the doorbell—a simple act, really, with the power to shatter a soul.

Marines are trained to kill. They are known for their blank stare and an allegiance to their unofficial motto, "No greater friend, no worse enemy." Since 2003, as the wars in Iraq and Afghanistan intensified, Marines such as Major Beck found themselves catapulted into a duty they never trained for—a mission without weapons.

As a Marine the forty-year-old had already won accolades as the most accomplished marksman of his class. He later earned two master's degrees in a quest to become a leader on the battlefield. He had hoped to deploy during the Persian Gulf War but was still in training when the conflict ended. He then trained and led Marines in preparations for conflicts in Somalia, Bosnia, and Haiti at the Marine Air Ground Task Force Training Command in Twentynine Palms, California. During the attacks of September 11, 2001, he served as a recruiter for the war he ached to join. During the initial invasion of Iraq, he was finishing his term at the Air Command and Staff College, hoping to transfer quickly to a deploying unit. Instead, he was sent to Colorado where he once again trained Marine reservists for war, expecting that he would soon join them.

He found himself faced with an assignment that starts with a long walk to a stranger's porch and an outstretched hand sheathed in a soft white glove. It continues with a promise steeped in the history of the Corps that most people associate only with the battlefield: Never leave a Marine behind.

In combat, men have taken bullets while retrieving their comrades' bodies, knowing that the dead Marine would have done the same for them. It is a tradition instilled in boot camp where Marines are ingrained with 230 years of history and the sacrifices of tens of thousands of lives.

For Major Beck—and thousands of men and women throughout the world tasked with notification duty—it is a promise that holds long after the dead return home.

Ask a Marine. Even the "grunts" on the front lines say they would rather be in the danger zone in Iraq than have to stand on that porch. From the beginning, Major Beck decided, if he was going to have to do it, he would do it his way, the way he would want it done if he were the one in the casket.

Over the next two years and through several notifications, Beck made a point of learning each dead Marine's name and nickname. He touched the toys they grew up with and read the letters they wrote home. He held grieving mothers in long embraces, absorbing their muffled cries into the dark blue shoulder of his uniform. Sometimes he returned home to his own family and cried in the dark.

When he first donned the Marine uniform, Steve Beck had never heard the term *casualty assistance calls officer*. He certainly never expected to serve as one. As it turned out, it would become the most important mission of his life.

As Veterans Day slid into another blank date on the calendar, the Marines drove through the snowy streets of the Laramie neighborhood. The house found them first, beckoning with the brightest porch lights and biggest address numbers on the block. Inside the SUV, the major played out scenarios with his gunnery sergeant as if they were headed into battle. *What if the parents aren't home? What if they become aggressive? What if they break down? What if, what if, what if?*

The major pulled to the curb and cut his headlights. He looked at the gunnery sergeant. Then the two men climbed out of the truck, walked on the untouched powder, and heard the soft snow crunch.

From then on every step would leave footprints.

In the basement of their home in Laramie, Kyle Burns's parents didn't hear the doorbell. The couple had spent most of the snowy night trying to hook up a new television. It was nearly 1:00 A.M. when the dog leaped into a barking frenzy. Kyle's mother climbed the stairs from the basement, looked out the window, and saw the two Marines on the frozen porch.

Go away! she thought. *Get the hell away from here!* Then she started screaming.

. . .

WHILE EACH DOOR is different, the scenes inside are almost always the same. "The curtains pull away. They come to the door. And they know. They always know," Major Beck said. "You can almost see the blood run out of their body and their heart hit the floor. It's not the blood as much as their soul. Something sinks. I've never seen that except when someone dies. And I've seen a lot of death.

"They're falling—either literally or figuratively—and you have to catch them. In this business I can't save his life. All I can do is catch the family while they're falling."

2

Navy Corpsman HM3 Christopher "Doc" Anderson

Longmont, Colorado

A NAVY CORPSMAN LOOKED at the blue star in the window and the name underneath, and felt his entire body wince. As a hazy winter sunset draped the foothills in the suburbs of Longmont, Colorado, the eyes of Navy Chief Petty Officer Kip "Doc" Poggemeyer fixed on the blue star flag, signifying the family had a loved one overseas. CHRISTOPHER A. "DOC" ANDERSON, the flag's stitching read.

The star tradition began during World War I when families would hang a blue star in the window of homes with a serviceman deployed overseas. A gold star meant he didn't make it back alive.

A year earlier, Doc Poggemeyer's wife had one of those flags in her window, as did his parents. Only the name was different.

Poggemeyer had spent his deployment at Marine Corps Air Station Al Asad in Iraq, the closest medical base to some of the heaviest fighting in the country—a base that frequently shook with mortar attacks. In his first week he saw massive combat wounds while performing the same job that his grandfather had held during World War II, the same job he knew he had wanted since he was a little boy.

Unlike Major Beck, he had seen the effects of combat "in country." He had watched men die. He tried not to think about the sailors who had to deliver the news back home.

That afternoon the corpsman and another casualty assistance officer first met a Navy chaplain. Together the sailors drove down the street, searching for the address. Each home they passed was one more where life would go on—homes where families sat down for dinner, made plans for the holidays, discussed the arrangement of their Christmas lights.

The SUV stopped in front of the home with an American flag flying from the porch, and the blue star flag that was about to turn gold. Doc Poggemeyer walked to the porch, pushed the doorbell, and felt as though a horse had kicked him in the stomach.

Debra Anderson opened the door, saw the men in uniform, and smiled. "Oh, honey," she said, calling to her husband. "The sailors are here. The recruiters are here."

Rick Anderson came to the stairs, and his face fell. A former Navy SEAL, he recognized the uniforms.

"Honey, we need to sit down," he said. "These aren't recruiters."

.   .   .

THE HISTORY OF the Navy hospital corpsman dates back to the Spanish-American War. The Marines needed a field medic and looked to the Navy to provide one. Since then, each time a Marine is wounded, he or she has turned to the sailor whose uniform is stitched with a caduceus — the well-known symbol of two intertwined snakes on a winged staff often used as an emblem for healers.

Navy corpsmen have served in some of the most harrowing battles of the last century. They have earned a disproportionate share of accolades and awards, and suffered a similarly large percentage of casualties.

Despite both services operating beneath the umbrella of the Navy, Marines and sailors hold an intense traditional rivalry. When new hospital corpsmen are assigned to Marine units, the Marines may tease them, calling them "squids" or worse. Still, the hospital corpsmen have to learn to think, act, and react with the speed of their Marine unit. Sometimes they are forced to grab a weapon. Before that, they are usually the ones reaching for the first aid kit.

When a hospital corpsman is first attached to a unit, the Marines will call the sailor by his or her last name, or maybe just "corpsman." Eventually, when sailors earn the Marines' respect, they are called "doc." Once the fighting begins, the corpsman's duty is usually one of the riskiest — corpsmen carry their own weapons along with loads of medical gear. The Marines say they will take a bullet for the corpsman because he or she is the only one who can take it out.

Somewhere near Ramadi, Christopher Anderson's Marines had called on their doc. Hours later, near Denver, Doc Poggemeyer received a similar call, one he hadn't prepared for in field medical training school.

A corpsman, he was told, had been killed in action (KIA) in Ramadi from a mortar attack. The doc had come full circle.

THAT NIGHT, TWENTY-TWO-YEAR-OLD Kyle Anderson steered his food delivery truck along the crumbly gravel roads of eastern Colorado. His cell phone rang, and he heard his father's voice asking him to come home, saying that he needed help with something. It was the first time in Kyle's life that he heard a waver in his father's voice. After serving in the Navy's most elite team of special forces and later earning a black belt in karate, there was nothing the old man couldn't handle.

Kyle asked the question that immediately consumed him: "Is my brother alive?"

"No," his father finally managed, and Kyle hung up the phone. On the other end of the line, his parents worried. The notification team offered to pick up the young man who was suddenly the couple's only son. When Kyle called back, his parents asked him to pull over. The sailors would meet him and help him drive back. He parked his truck near an intersection just off the interstate and waited, crying alone in the dark.

Is this really happening? he wondered. As he waited longer, he thought, *Maybe they won't show up.*

When the sailors arrived, Kyle dropped his head. He got out of the car and stepped into the stinging 25-degree wind, his tears freezing on his cheeks.

Along the nearby interstate, cars rushed past at 75 miles per hour. They did not slow down.

3

Marine Second Lieutenant
James J. Cathey

Brighton, Colorado, and Reno, Nevada

O N A BLUE SKY Labor Day weekend in a new upscale residential neighborhood, a middle-aged man mowed his yard as a silver SUV ambled down the street past manicured lawns and half-finished homes. In a place filled with soccer moms and SUVs, the Suburban with government plates didn't stick out. The two men inside did. Daylight notifications can be tricky. The sight of men in formal uniforms can set off alarms in every military family in the neighborhood. At night the truck can slip through the streets like a scythe.

Minutes before, as they temporarily parked outside the neighborhood, the two men bowed their heads.

Major Beck and Navy chaplain Jim Chapman closed their eyes

in prayer as the chaplain asked for "words that will bring the family peace."

At the time, Major Beck didn't know what those words would be. He never does.

Two Marines are required for each death notification, not just for emotional support but for each other's protection. While most parents eventually grow close to their casualty assistance calls officer, the initial meeting tests all emotions. Major Beck likens it to the first exposure a baby chick has when it opens its eyes. That connection, that bond, he says, will never break.

At the beginning of the war in Iraq, one of the Marines from the major's unit was slapped by a furious mother. In 2004 a distraught father in Florida set fire to a van that carried the Marines sent to notify him.

When the knock came, Katherine Cathey was napping in her bedroom. Her stepfather saw the Marines first.

"We're here for Katherine," the major said quietly.

"Oh, no," Vic Leonard said.

At first Katherine's mother thought it was a salesman. Then she saw her husband walking backward and the two men in uniform.

"Oh, no," she said, and then, "She's pregnant!"

Vic asked his wife to wake up Katherine. Vicki Leonard shook her head. She couldn't speak.

When her stepfather opened the door to her bedroom, Katherine could hear her mother crying—no, *wailing*. She had never heard her mother cry like that.

"What's going on?" Katherine asked her stepfather.

"It's not good," he told her. "Come with me."

Her own screams began as soon as she saw the uniforms.

Katherine ran to the back of the living room and collapsed on the floor, holding her pregnant stomach and thinking of the man who would never see their baby. Finally she stood, but she still couldn't speak. As the major and the chaplain remained on their feet, she glared at them. It was a stare the major had seen before, the one that hurts the most.

The pregnant woman ran to the back of the house and drew a hot bath. For the next hour she sat in the tub, dissolving.

As the chaplain looked over the family, Major Beck ducked back outside to make a quick phone call.

Inside an SUV in Reno, Nevada, just around the corner from the home where Jim Cathey grew up, another military cell phone rang.

THE TOOL CABINET was a mess.

Jim Cathey's mother stood in the garage in Reno, trying to find the right wrench to fix a sprinkler head in her front yard. Then the dog began barking, and she had to bring him inside. Her husband had left that morning on a long drive, scouting his favorite hunting ground.

What a frustrating morning, she thought as she gave up on looking for the wrench. She would have to make a quick trip to the hardware store.

When the SUV pulled up, the Marines inside assumed someone was home—after all, a lawn mower sat outside and a sprinkler head was exposed, leaving a job unfinished. Maybe the parents had just stepped inside. The Marines made the long walk. No one answered the door.

They retreated to the vehicle. A neighbor drove up, glanced at the Marines, and pulled into an adjacent driveway. Once inside, the neighbor looked out a window at them. The Marines shifted in their seats—as if they weren't uncomfortable enough already.

When Caroline Cathey drove up, she saw the government vehicle that didn't belong on the street and then fixed her eyes on the man in the driver's seat.

"Time to go," Captain Winston Tierney said.

Caroline Cathey's hands went to her face.

Tierney and his men walked quickly to the woman, who looked as if she might faint. The captain tried to give her a hug, supporting her weight.

"Please don't let it be," she said.

"I'm sorry to have to be here today. Can we go inside and sit down? There are some things we need to confirm."

"Please tell me it's not Jimmy. Please tell me it's not my son."

The Marines stayed with the Catheys for the next ten hours. With Caroline's help they contacted Jim Cathey's nine-year-old daughter, Casey, who was born while he was still in high school. Like many Marines, Cathey had already lived a complicated and at times rudderless life before entering the Corps. Along with the child he had fathered while still a boy, he also married and divorced another woman who was not the mother of the child—long before he met Katherine. Still, when the time came to pin on his lieutenant's bars at the most important ceremony of his life, he chose Casey and Katherine to pin the rank on his shoulder.

A few hours after the Marines showed up at the Catheys' door, young Casey's mother and stepfather drove the girl from Carson City, Nevada, to Reno where another one of the Marines—an operations chief who had children of his own—told her that her daddy had been hurt in the war and wouldn't be able to come back. He asked her if she understood. She answered with tears.

Meanwhile, the Marines had contacted the state police to look for Jeff Cathey, Jim's father, since they knew he suffered from clinical depression and would take the news especially hard.

Late that night, Jeff Cathey pulled into his driveway and saw the Marines at the door. He heard their message and then drove to the home of his parents, who lived only a few blocks away. The family would take it from there.

When it was all over, the exhausted Marines climbed back into the silver SUV. A staff sergeant looked at Captain Tierney.

"Sir," he said, "please don't take me on another one of these."

4

Marine Corporal Brett Lee Lundstrom

Black Hawk, South Dakota

SURROUNDED BY THE land that once rooted her, not far from the Pine Ridge Indian Reservation, Doyla Lundstrom's cell phone flashed with a message. She asked her fiancé, John Hauk, to check the call. A neighbor was trying to contact Doyla, and she asked her fiancé to call back. The woman told him that she wanted to speak to Doyla but then said it could wait until she got home.

During her two sons' deployments to Afghanistan and Iraq, Doyla would often pause at the stop sign near her house, peering down the street, looking for vehicles that didn't belong. Each night the chaplain wasn't at her door, she went to sleep saying, "That was a good day."

This night something felt wrong. Somebody was trying to hide something from her, and she knew it. As she drove, she asked for the phone to call the neighbor back.

"Did my house burn down?" she asked the neighbor. "Is there a problem with the dog?"

No, the neighbor told her, none of that. It could wait until she got home.

Doyla's first language is Lakota. She grew up on the Pine Ridge reservation, but her mother died when she was ten years old, leaving her with a father who found a new wife and drank much of the time. She left the reservation as a teenager for a foster home. She met a cute guy named Ed Lundstrom, who grew up on the nearby Rosebud Indian Reservation. Soon after high school, Ed enlisted in the Marine Corps, taking them both away from the only land they knew and into a different kind of warrior culture.

For much of the family's life it was just Doyla and their two sons, living primarily in New Jersey and Virginia while their father was away on officer training and deployments to Cuba and the Persian Gulf. When he arrived home, they trekked to historic battlefields, where the boys memorized the history and made plans to become part of it.

Although he had only limited knowledge of his heritage, Brett Lundstrom always said he wanted to be a Marine. When he was a teenager, he told his friends, "I will die for you." On September 11, 2001, the family lived in New Jersey, thirty-five miles from ground zero, and his mother knew it wouldn't be long before her sons joined the fight. She persuaded Brett to try college for a year. At the same time, after nearly three decades, Doyla and Ed's marriage began to crumble. Not long afterward, Brett enlisted, followed by his younger brother, Eddy.

Even after Brett returned home from boot camp, she still called him by his nickname, "Brettlee." Eddy was always "Babyson." In one family photo of Eddy in his Army uniform, relatives say he looks exactly like his grandfather, who fought with the Army in Korea. The family tradition of warriors goes back generations, to the famed Lakota chief Red Cloud.

Brett was the outgoing big brother who called his mother three or four times a day, and they talked like teenage girls, sharing everything—to the point where his friends would say, "Dude, I can't believe you told your mom *that*."

Eddy was always the quiet one, more like his father, introspective.

Brett served three months in Afghanistan in 2004. Nine months later, in September 2005, he headed to Iraq with the Second Battalion, Sixth Marines, Second Marine Division. Like many military kids who moved around most of their lives, the strapping six-foot-two Marine with the wide grin had no problem making new friends.

On one of his last nights visiting Colorado, Brett spent the night in the same room as his thirteen-year-old cousin, Richard Munoz. Before he crashed on the couch that night, Richard said the Marine told him, "Live life while you can." Then he fell asleep.

. . .

CALL IT MOTHER'S intuition, Doyla says. Call it a Lakota feeling. She couldn't wait. As she drove home that night, she asked her fiancé to call the neighbor one more time.

"Call her back and ask her if the chaplain came to the door," she said.

By then, young Marines throughout the country called Doyla Lundstrom "Ma." Her home in Virginia was always open to the boys' friends. Sometimes it was party central, with Doyla watching over them. Sometimes it was a refuge to escape their own problems. For many it was their home away from home—the one Doyla never had, a haven overseen by a mother who could barely remember hers.

Her fiancé dialed the neighbor's phone number.

"Did the chaplain come to the door?"

Doyla knew by his expression what was said on the other end of the line. She pulled the car over, took the phone, and called the boys' father, who lived in Detroit. The men in uniform had already come to his door. When he answered the phone, Ed Lundstrom was crying, choking on the words.

"Which one was it?" she asked, but he was too overcome to answer.

She screamed into the telephone: "*Which one was it?*"

For what seemed like several minutes he couldn't speak.

"That was the worst of it all, right there," she said later. "Those moments of not knowing which one it was."

5

Army Private First Class
Jesse A. Givens

Fountain, Colorado

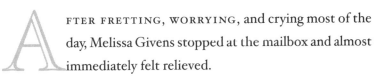FTER FRETTING, WORRYING, and crying most of the day, Melissa Givens stopped at the mailbox and almost immediately felt relieved.

"Melissa, hey angel," began her husband's letter from Iraq.

That morning she had heard about a grenade attack that might have involved soldiers from the nearby Army base at Fort Carson—an area where local stores advertise "maps of Pikes Peak, Colorado Springs, and Baghdad," a place where the ubiquitous magnetic SUPPORT OUR TROOPS yellow ribbons on the cars are more than popular platitudes. Here they are backed up by bumper stickers that read HALF MY HEART IS IN IRAQ. It is a town where pickup windows are regularly marked in shoe polish that read MY DADDY IS MY HERO or MY MAN IS COMING HOME! It's also a place where the schoolchildren have learned to dread the sight of television trucks at the gate to the base: It means one of their classmates likely just lost a parent.

Melissa felt the stress all morning. She was pregnant with a baby she knew only as Bean, because that's what the fetus looked like on the last sonogram Jesse Givens saw before he left for war. Meanwhile, she had to keep herself together for her five-year-old son, Dakota, whom her husband playfully called Toad.

She opened the letter and read it in the car. *These are his words*, she thought. *He must be all right.*

> *I'm writing you letters and sending them but I don't know if you're getting them. . . . I tell you this place sucks. Hey if anybody asks if they should send me anything tell them an American flag. Melissa I miss you every day. I think, worry and pray for you. I feel like a huge hole has been cut into my soul. I want so bad to hug you. I want to listen to your breath beside me while I sleep.*

Following the instructions from the letter, they bought an American flag to send to Iraq and then headed for the grocery store. Out of nowhere, Dakota asked where falling stars came from. It was a conversation she would never shake. Before leaving for Iraq, Jesse had asked her to go out at night and look up at the stars. He told her he would be looking at the same stars, focusing on the brightest one, and if she couldn't sleep, she should start to count them. It was how he ended all his letters: Count the stars.

Please don't get used to me being gone [his letter continued].
*I am sorry I'm not there with you right now. I know it doesn't
seem like it all the time, but I tried to be there when you really
needed me. Usually I can make it happen, but there was no way to
get out of this. I guess this way at least I can give you and Toad
and Bean food and a home.*

Jesse had also included a separate note for Dakota. It came
with a sketch of a scorpion and a reference to the boy's security
blanket, Mr. Blankie.

As Dakota grew up, he would drag the blanket everywhere,
Linus-like, and as it inevitably shed loose threads, Jesse would
pick them off the floor and braid them together. When he left for
Iraq, he took the ragged Mr. Blankie braid with him.

In the letter, Jesse Givens said he wanted Dakota to know that
even in Iraq his son's security blanket still worked.

Dakota,

*I saw a scorpion today. Do you know what a scorpion is? It's a
big bug with pinchers and a poisoned tail. . . . He was scary looking. I had my piece of Mr. Blankie with me so I'm sure that is what
protected me. I miss you a lot. You know you are the best boy in the
world. I hope you are alright, I worry about you all the time. I
can't wait to come home and give you bellyfishes (tickles). I love
you son. Don't forget to say your prayers and dream about us at the
park. Love always, Dad*

After returning home to the barren two-room apartment the family could barely afford on Jesse's Army private's salary, Melissa read the note to Dakota, put away the groceries, and relaxed on the couch. As she finally had a chance to rest, she felt a wave of calm and turned on the television.

It was May 1, 2003. On the television screen, the president of the United States prepared to land on an aircraft carrier where he would declare an end to major combat operations in Iraq.

Okay, the war is over, Melissa thought. *He's going to come home.*

As she watched the coverage, Dakota asked to play outside, and she left her door open so she could hear him. On the television, newscasters were still talking about the president's address to the nation when she looked up and saw the men in Army uniforms at the open door. One of them leaned in and knocked.

She looked up and the man in green asked if she was Mrs. Gibbons. She told him no. It was Givens, not Gibbons. Then he said, "Are you Melissa?" She nodded, and he began to read the paper as if it were a script for an audition he hadn't rehearsed. He kept stumbling, but she managed to make out, "The Army regrets to inform you . . ."

The officers told her that her husband died after his tank had crashed through a berm and fell into a canal off the Euphrates River. The rest of the crew escaped through a hatch, but Jesse was trapped inside.

Of all the dangers they were warned about, of all the terrible scenarios that went through the minds of his family, it was a scene nobody imagined: Pfc. Jesse A. Givens drowned in the desert.

Melissa didn't believe it. She argued with the men, saying there was no water in the desert. How could he possibly have drowned? First they got her last name wrong, and then this. She decided to make the soldiers a deal. Since it was all a big mistake, she told them, they could leave and she would promise not to tell anyone in the Army that they had come. That way, they wouldn't get in trouble.

It couldn't be true, she insisted. She had just read his own words in the letter.

Well, I better go for now. It may be a while before we can make phone calls. But I will continue to write as much as possible. I love you. Give Toad and Bean hugs and kisses. Count the stars. Love your husband, Jess.

LONG AFTER THE Army men left and Melissa was alone, she began looking through the stacks of black-and-white college composition books where Jesse had scrawled his thoughts and sketches. She was looking for more of his words of comfort, smearing them with her tears.

25 Nov. 2002

I am not going to pretend that I understand why we are thinking about going to war with Iraq. I know the reasons you have given—

some seem more credible than others. No matter what the reasons, I will go and fight with all my heart. Not to win a war, but to come home to my wife and my children. I took an oath to protect my country. Not for the sake of saving the world, but for the hopes that my family wouldn't have to live in a world filled with hate, fear and sadness—a world which America was exposed to on Sept. 11, 2001. If we are involved in combat and I fall, who will raise my children? Who will be there for my wife? I sacrifice not only my life, but a husband and a father's life also. Who will see that my wife can support my children through all of their years? Who will provide my family with their basic needs? I didn't ask for your pity or money, I just ask that we do this for the right reasons. I ask that when you send soldiers into battle, that they are not just numbers. I ask that you see our roles as fathers, sons, daughters, wives and husbands—as well as seen as the proud Americans who want to serve our country. When all is said and done, will we, the United States military, shed blood or pass at the hands of our enemies for a just cause? Will you remember those who we leave behind and honor them as well as our fallen brothers and sisters?

PART 2

REVERBERATIONS

You always hear all these statements like "freedom isn't free."
You hear the president talking about all these people making
sacrifices. But you never really know until you carry one of
them in the casket. When you feel their body weight.
When you feel them, that's when you know.
That's when you understand.

—MARINE STAFF SERGEANT KEVIN THOMAS

6

Red Platoon

Fallujah, Iraq

O N THE MORNING of Veterans Day, 2004, politicians appeared on morning talk shows, cemetery workers and American Legion posts prepared for their annual ceremonies, and various stores advertised their red-white-and-blue-tinted sales for mattresses and used cars.

In Iraq, amid the ruins of Fallujah, the insurgents opened fire.

"Marine hit," the radio crackled. "I think he's hurt pretty bad."

As the Marines of Red Platoon moved to rush the injured man to a hospital, the gunfire intensified, along with rocket-propelled grenades. More than any other time in his life, First Lieutenant Paul Webber thought he was about to die. "I was so heavily engaged, I couldn't withdraw without exposing myself worse," he later recalled. "That's when Kyle was hit, and all hell broke loose."

Within minutes a rocket-propelled grenade sliced into the right side of Lance Corporal Kyle Burns, a Carhartt-wearing, Copenhagen-chewing, hard-swearing, churchgoing kid from Laramie.

The twenty-year-old had squirreled tins of chewing tobacco all around the Humvee, packing them into every cranny. He still carried his fishing license in his wallet.

Not far away, a staff sergeant from Littleton, Colorado, received the call to roll in. At six-foot-two and 230 pounds, twenty-seven-year-old Sam Holder was built like the old G.I. Joe action figures, with a square jaw, massive muscles, and a tree-trunk chest that tapered to a trim waist.

Although relatively new to the unit, Staff Sergeant Holder had earned the respect of even the lowest-ranking Marines, with a wisecracking sense of humor and a reputation for unflinching, decisive action.

As they stood in the turret, Staff Sergeant Holder and his gunner were exposed from the waist up, protected only by body armor.

Once the Marines on foot pulled the injured man into their vehicle, Staff Sergeant Holder relayed the order to pull forward and divert attention away from the makeshift ambulance for the injured Marine.

First Lieutenant Webber listened over the radio as Staff Sergeant Holder's vehicle moved toward the insurgents.

"He pulled up in front of the vehicle that was stuck there, and he became a bullet sponge for all the fire that was being directed there," the platoon leader said. "He was hit, but he still stayed on his machine gun. That allowed the platoon to break contact. While he was laying down the fire, he was dying, and I think he knew it. It was by far the most courageous act that I have ever witnessed. He died for his buddies."

THE NAMES OF the dead Marines were soon relayed to the United States, resulting in the inevitable insistence of the knock. In Denver, as Major Beck began his trek through the blizzard in Wyoming, the leader of the Red Platoon stood in a sweltering house occupied by coalition forces in Fallujah and began a task that would also haunt him. The house was dark. The room was quiet. He faced the men and began to speak.

He couldn't see their faces—only silhouettes of Marines—and he managed to muster the words: "Staff Sergeant Holder and Lance Corporal Burns passed away on the way to Bravo Surgical in Camp Fallujah."

He heard a whimper from the dark. Hours earlier, some of the two Marines' best friends had mopped the blood from the Humvees.

First Lieutenant Webber told the men to try to get some sleep. Then he walked through the house and sat alone at an Iraqi dinner table. There he began to write an account of what had happened. Much of it would end up on the citations for Kyle Burns's Navy and Marine Corps Commendation Medal with "V" for valor and for Sam Holder's Silver Star.

Like most of the other Marines, the first lieutenant then swept the day as far back as possible, focusing instead on the mission. Eventually, he could no longer hold back.

"I feel like if I don't get this out I'm going to explode. So bear with me," he later wrote in an e-mail to his fiancée, Brooke Faschetti, whom he later married.

> *Sometimes I feel like I'm going to lose it. Maybe it's good that I recognize this now and am trying to do something. My mind races and I can't sleep. Some days I'm OK but most not. I feel shaky, depressed, confused. What happened on the 11th keeps replaying through my head. I have to keep telling myself I wasn't the one who killed them, it was the enemy. I remember Burns and how limp he was when I pulled him out of the turret—how white his skin was. Looking over as everything was falling apart and seeing Staff Sgt. Holder slumped down in his turret, blood all over his flak. I don't know why I'm still here. . . . I still feel as if I have blood on my hands. This will never go away. Will it?*

When Brooke wrote him back, she did her best to help him answer that question.

> *The thing is this: You should not ever forget what happened. Because what happened to you and those men is something absolutely worthy and precious of remembering and holding close to*

your heart. It is part of who you are and who you will grow to become. What you also need to realize is that while this will always be there with you . . . eventually that will be OK. That while the blood feels still fresh on your hands . . . eventually it will be in your heart and it will touch your soul.

7

Major Steve Beck

Aurora, Colorado

MOMENTS AFTER MAJOR Beck's phone rang with the news, he felt the pressure of the clock. Once the call is received, the goal for notification is four hours.

Troops in the battle zone often have access to e-mail and satellite telephones now, so when a service member dies, the area is placed under "River City," or R.C. When an area goes R.C., all communication back home is shut off to keep rumors from reaching the family before the notification officers arrive. Still, Major Beck knew that bad news runs like water downhill, creating its own path.

"As soon as we receive the call," Major Beck said, "we are racing the electron."

The call often comes in the middle of the night. Officers must retrieve vital information from headquarters—the Marine's next of kin, the basic circumstances surrounding the death, addresses and phone numbers—and there is no room for error.

During World War I, World War II, and the Korean War, notification arrived in sparse sympathy letters or in the terse language of telegrams, leaving relatives alone to soak in the words. Near the end of the Vietnam War, the military changed the process, saddling stateside troops with the knock at the door.

When he began the job as site commander at Marine Air Control Squadron 23, Major Beck knew that death notification was a possibility. The previous commander had already supervised three funerals in the region that includes Colorado and parts of Wyoming, Kansas, South Dakota, and Nebraska.

Until that first call, however, he had plenty of other worries. From their base among the top-secret radar installations at Buckley Air Force Base near Denver, Major Beck and his Marines were highly trained to support aircraft and missile operations. They also are continually trained Marine reservists, preparing them for stints in Iraq, Afghanistan, and Africa.

DIFFERENT SERVICES HAVE different guidelines for notification. In the Army, one officer is responsible for the knock while another steps in to handle the aftercare. In the Marine Corps, the same person who knocks on the door is the family's primary contact for the next year or more.

For Major Beck that continual contact is crucial. Once he makes the knock, he says, he is eternally linked to that family.

"As soon as they see you, freeze frame—*pchew*," he said, imitating the sound of a camera flash. "You'll never forget it. It locks in."

It is a moment that he says never gets easier. He knows that some families will blame the messenger. At times he does, too.

"I can't help but feel that I'm the person who's bringing them all that pain," he said. "Maybe that's what hurts me the most: that because I'm standing in front of them, they're feeling as bad as they're ever going to feel."

8

Sergeant Andrew "Andy" Alonzo

Fort Logan National Cemetery, Denver, Colorado

AMONG THE FIELDS covered in the stubble of gray marble markers, Fort Logan National Cemetery caretakers store a stack of headstones with no names.

A week after Veterans Day, 2004, just outside a small work shed at the edge of the cemetery, Sergeant Andrew Alonzo—call him Andy, he says—smoothed his hands over two stone slabs. In the morning sunlight they remained cold to the touch.

"All I know is that they're for two Marines, both killed on Veterans Day. One was from Colorado, one from Wyoming. Killed on the same day, in the same area."

In a few days the Marines would be buried within a few yards of each other, the first time since the Vietnam War that the cemetery would hold two funerals on the same day for men killed in action.

Five days before the burials, Andy picked out two slabs of marble, each cut to the same specifications: four feet long and weighing roughly 240 pounds. The markers are kept in a cardboard box labeled "Blanks," reserved specifically for soldiers killed in action. The cemetery had just received a new shipment.

"They look the same, but they're very different," the forty-two-year-old said of the two marble slabs—one from Georgia and the other from Mississippi. "You can see the differences in color. You can see it in the marble. If you know where to look, you can see the differences."

Fort Logan generally receives the headstones already emblazoned with the name of the deceased. They are ordered directly from the quarry and set in place a month or two after the funeral. For troops killed in action, however, cemetery workers like to set the headstones on the same day as the burial. To ensure that the task is done on time, the stones must be smoothed, cleaned, and prepared on-site. The process begins with a blank slate.

Inside the workshop, Andy slid a long steel file across one of the headstones, filling the room with white powdery smoke and the grinding rhythm of metal on marble.

"I wonder what they were like," he said, staring at the headstones. "Sometimes, you try to visualize them."

More than a year earlier, Andy lost one of his own comrades in Iraq; they had both served in the Sunni Triangle. At times he still wrestles with the loss, and at one point he even considered suicide.

Then he found solace among the familiar terrain of Fort Logan, alongside the headstones he set himself, to honor men and women he never knew.

That morning he began his journey to mark the lives of two more. "When the headstones are blank, there's something missing, just something missing," Andy said. "It's like the names are just floating out there, waiting. They're waiting for the stone."

AFTER RETURNING FROM Iraq, Andy measured his time by the new white marble markers set on the hill atop the graves of veterans who had fought in the wars before his.

"When I left for Iraq, none of these were here," he said, pointing to the graves—an average of fifteen a day, dug primarily for World War II veterans—while he served as a member of the Colorado-based 244th Engineer Battalion of the Army Reserve.

"Now we have two more coming," he said, nodding toward the area where the new arrivals would be buried.

Nearly all the groundskeepers at the national cemetery are veterans. Andy joined the Marines after graduating from high school in a small town in southeastern Colorado and spent the next "thirteen years, one month, and two weeks" in the Corps. Caught in the force reductions and base closures of the 1990s, he took early retirement and then worked as an orderly at a Department of Veterans' Affairs hospital.

He started digging graves at Fort Logan in 1998 and worked his way to a supervisory position. He was called to go to Iraq in March 2003. He received his orders while working at the cemetery.

Six months after returning, he viewed the headstones from his electric golf cart and spotted something nobody else could see. He hit the brake.

"These stones," he said, pointing to a row that was slightly askew. "Look at them."

After more than twenty years in the military, he was specially tuned to cracks in uniformity. In his closet at home, all his shirts face the same way; they are in order from long to short. He can tell if someone has moved something in his house, for example, if it is not dead center on the table. Every implement in his toolbox has its place.

"And I'm the same way with headstones," he said. "If I see something out of place I'll make 'em pull it out and do it again."

Although he had served overseas in noncombat zones, Andy admits enduring emotional changes since coming home from Iraq as he struggled to cope with the memories.

"I have to take sleeping pills, but my body keeps fighting them, so they have to increase the dosage," he said. "Now the dreams are getting further apart."

Since returning, he doesn't trust people the way he used to, he said. He jumps at the rifle salutes that jolt the cemetery periodically during the day, and he still drops his head when taps drifts through the field.

Other things have changed, too. He always sits with his back to the wall in restaurants. When driving, he scans the road for debris, still programmed to look for improvised explosive devices.

He does not think he is as social as he once was. And now he cries during war movies.

"I never used to cry like that," he said.

Before he deployed, he never used to miss the news on the war. Now he tries to avoid it. Inevitably, it finds him in his cemetery.

O N THE MORNING the headstones were scheduled to receive their names, a graying Vietnam vet entered the workshop. The name on his drab work shirt read WALT. Ever since Andy asked Walter Huling to haul the blank stones into the shop the day before, the lanky fifty-eight-year-old couldn't stop thinking of them.

"I want to see them put the names on," Walt said as he waited for the engraver to arrive. "When they're blank like this, you never know. You think, 'It could be my name on there.' "

In Vietnam, Walt survived two helicopter crashes and earned a Bronze Star for making it through a two-day firefight where half his company was killed. Once he watched as the men on either side of him were shot, but he survived.

"The first thing I did in Vietnam was police the bodies of dead Marines to put them in the body bags," Walt said. "I was nineteen. Like to scare a young man to death. It was a sight you never forget. But it also taught me an appreciation for life. That it could be me lying there."

He looked out at the headstones.

"It's life and death every day out here. When you work out here, you take advantage of life as life is."

Back at the blank stones, the engraver arrived from a local funeral company and laid out the templates with the names of the two Marines in capital letters. Andy and Walt read them aloud:

KYLE W. BURNS

THEODORE SAMUEL HOLDER II

They calculated the ages in their heads, which they had learned to do instantly, and Walt pounded his chest. "One of them is the same age as my son," he said.

Together, the two men wondered aloud whether the dead Marines knew each other and whether they were killed in the same battle. As the engraver sandblasted the names into the marble, Andy looked up. "With the names there, you start to get a clearer picture of them," he said. "The names aren't floating around in the air anymore."

The Vietnam veteran nodded. "Let it be written," he said. "Once it's written in stone, that's it. Let it be written in stone."

9

Major Steve Beck

Aurora, Colorado

As Andy Alonzo prepared the gravesites for the two Marines killed on Veterans Day, Major Beck tended to the family of Kyle Burns in Wyoming. At the same time, other Marines from his detachment comforted the family of Sam Holder in a Denver suburb.

As casualties mounted, the Colorado Marines couldn't even take their uniforms to the dry cleaners because they had to dash to another funeral fraught with concern that they might be summoned to knock at another door. They kept their dress blues in the back of the car, pressed and ready. Major Beck took to carrying a collection of lint rollers in the car as a substitute for the cleaners. Before one notification, he changed in the bathroom of an Olive Garden restaurant—entering as a civilian and exiting in uniform. He shakes off Superman comparisons. It is just the opposite, he says.

Despite the public's perception, there is no group of service members whose primary task is death notification. Just as every Marine is a rifleman, expected to grab a weapon and head to the front if called upon, any mid-level ranking Marine could also be called to knock on the door.

Imagine such a scenario in the civilian world, Major Beck says. Imagine an accountant, a plumber, or a lawyer being pulled out of the office at any time and being directed to walk up to a stranger's door, tell him what nobody wants to hear, and then go back to work.

For Major Beck that door is the L.O.D., the line of departure, the point of no return.

After all the racing, all the frantic scramble, it is the point where time freezes.

"Once I get to the porch, I stand there and take a deep breath. At that point you can wait ten seconds, thirty seconds, or an hour. It's not going to go away," he said. "There's no option. There's no fork in the road. You just stare down that straight path. You step up because there is no fork.

"I pick myself up, gather my thoughts, and ring the bell."

10

Army Private First Class
Jesse A. Givens

Fountain, Colorado

MELISSA GIVENS BEGAN to hate the mailbox. For weeks the letters continued to come, but this time they were not conversational. This time they were good-byes—just in case.

I don't know if you will ever understand the light you brought into my life, reads one of the last letters written by Pfc. Jesse Givens. It was still stained by the muddy river in Iraq where he had died, smearing his handwriting, ripping apart his last words.

I want you to know I have every moment we ever spent together in my heart.

The second letter was found in his wallet—wet and wrinkled but fully intact—pressed against a tiny flower. It began with the end.

My angel, my wife, my love, my friend. If you're reading this, I won't be coming home. . . .

The final letter arrived a month after the funeral, memorial service, and gun salute. It came in the mail only days after Melissa gave birth to the baby her husband called the Bean.

Inside was Jesse Givens's final draft:

> *My family:*
>
> *I never thought I would be writing a letter like this, I really don't know where to start. I've been getting bad feelings though and well if you are reading this . . .*
>
> *I searched all my life for a dream and I found it in you. . . . The happiest moments in my life all deal with my little family. You will never know how complete you have made me. Each and every one of you. You saved me from loneliness and taught me how to think beyond myself. You taught me how to live and to love. You opened my eyes to a world I never even dreamed existed. . . .*

In her living room, the twenty-seven-year-old widow picked up the three letters that all attempted to say the same thing.

"He called me a week before it happened and told me he had written the letter but not to open it unless he died," Melissa Givens said. "When I got his personal effects, I found another letter. Then the other one came. They were backup letters. In case one letter didn't make it, he wanted to make sure we got one of the others," she said.

"But they were all good-byes."

Dakota, you are more son than I could ever ask for. I can only hope I was half the dad. You taught me how to care until it hurts, you taught me how to smile again. You taught me that life isn't so serious and sometimes you have to play. You have a big beautiful heart. Through life you need to keep it open and follow it. Never be afraid to be yourself. I will always be there in our park when you dream so we can still play together. I hope someday you will have a son like mine. Make them smile and shine just like you. I hope someday you will understand why I didn't come home. Please be proud of me. Please don't stop loving life. Take in every breath like it's your first. I will always be there with you. I'll be in the sun, shadows, dreams, and joys of your life.

Dakota was almost a year old when they met. With a single mispronounced word, the little boy sealed the relationship.

"I had dated other people since I had Dakota, but he didn't like any of them," Melissa said. "But when Jesse was here, [Dakota] went over and put his hand on Jesse's knee and said, 'You my danny.' That was his way of saying *daddy*. So I kept him. I figured, 'If the kid likes him, I'll keep him.'"

They met in 1999 as employees at ShopKo in Joplin, Missouri. Jesse worked security; Melissa was a cashier and a single mother. He was a big-hearted, thoughtful bookworm and budding artist. She was the opposite in just about every way.

"We pretty much had nothing in common. He liked to read, but if a book didn't have pictures, I wouldn't read it," she said, speaking in a Midwest drawl, pronouncing "pictures" as "pitchers."

"He was into his future and his life and his family, and I wanted to party and do my own thing." She smiled and shook her head. "He worshiped the quicksand I walked on."

The two moved in together, and he found a job as an ironworker. He helped raise Dakota and spent hours with him in the parks, building memories he would later ask the boy to remember in his dreams.

That life froze on September 11, 2001, as Givens watched his fellow ironworkers on television during the rescue effort in New York City. Within weeks he traded his hard hat for a soldier's helmet.

"He was watching it all, and he said, 'I should be there. I should be there,'" Melissa remembered. "And he was so patriotic. He thought that's the way we all should believe."

The couple married as soon as he returned from basic training, and the family moved to Fort Carson in 2002. Soon afterward — just as the rhetoric heated up between the United States and Iraq — Melissa found out she was pregnant.

"We heard they were going to get their orders in August 2002. But they kept putting it off, and we thought, 'Well, maybe they'll put it off until the baby's born,'" Melissa said. "Then on Valentine's Day they got the orders."

Bean, I never got to see you but I know in my heart you are beautiful. I will always have with me the feel of the soft nudges on your mom's belly, and the joy I felt when we found out you were on the way. I dream of you every night, and I always will. Don't ever think that since I wasn't around that I didn't love you. You

*were conceived of love and I came to this terrible place for love.
Please understand that I had to be gone so that I could take care
of my family. I love you Bean.*

In his mother's arms, ten-month-old Carson Givens raised his
eyebrows in a funny expression that Melissa recognized immediately
from the face she thought she would never see again. She calls the
expression "Jesse's eyebrow thing." It bothers her and comforts her.

"Da-da-da-da-da," the infant gurgled.

"Yes, you're saying, 'Da-da-daddy.' Yeah, he's up there," Melissa
said, pointing to a portrait on the wall. "Up there."

From the portrait, Jesse Givens still watches over the living room.

"Carson looks at the picture when we start talking about
[Jesse]," Melissa said. "He used to look at his brother and say, 'Da-
da-daddy,' but one day Dakota took him up to the picture and
said, 'No, I'm not your daddy. This is your daddy.' And he told him
a long story, that 'this is only a picture of your daddy. Your daddy
was killed in Iraq. He drowned in a tank.'

"Dakota told him, 'This is just a picture of your daddy, but he's
always in your heart.'"

IN THE BASEMENT, Jesse Givens's life is divided into two
steamer trunks: one for the boy he called Toad, and one for
the baby Bean.

"I want to save everything. I want the boys to see how good

he was at everything he did," Melissa said. "Whatever I can hold on to."

From Dakota's trunk she pulled out a dandelion blossom, which Jesse had flattened and laminated.

"Dakota gave him this one day. He had it in his wallet [when he died]," she said. "I didn't know he took it with him."

As she dug to the bottom of the trunk, Melissa found a piece of their lives before the war—Jesse's old ironworker's hard hat. On the back he had written two names: Toad and Angel.

"Toad is there because Dakota couldn't say his name when they first met. He could only say 'Toada.' So Jesse always called him Toad," Melissa said.

She paused.

"Angel is me," she finally said, "because he always thought I was his angel who saved him. But it was actually the other way around—he was mine because he fixed my life. I did some not-so-great things," she said, referring to her past with drugs, "and he took me away from all that. He showed me how to make good choices. He gave me Carson. And then he passed away. And I think that was what he was meant to do—to help me fix my life."

From one of the trunks she picked up a small white goose-down feather.

"Dakota and me decided that every time we see a feather like this, that means that an angel passed by," she said, smiling as she remembered another story:

"One night I fell asleep with Carson in my bed," she said, holding the feather.

That night Dakota had a bad dream, so he came in and curled up alongside them. During the night, the bedding shed several white down feathers, which stuck to the lotion on the infant's face. In the morning, Dakota woke up, looked at his baby brother, and awakened his mother.

"Dakota said, 'Look, Mommy,' and pointed to the feathers," Melissa said.

"He said, 'Daddy slept with us last night.' "

MELISSA SENT SEVERAL letters to her husband. They all remain in the basement, returned by the military, unopened.

"The only one he got was the one I gave him in person on the day he left," she said.

That first and final letter from Melissa arrived with his personal belongings, neatly packaged with his good-bye letters. Like many of his possessions, it was sealed by the Army in a clear plastic sleeve that Melissa was instructed not to open, since it may have come in contact with dangerous chemicals inside the tank.

Since she can't open the protective sleeve, she can only read the first side:

Jesse. My baby. Since I know you like letters so much I figured I would start writing before you left so you would have something to read until I could write again. There are some things I need to make sure that you know. . . . Don't worry. You did what you did to take care of us. I want you to know that no matter how this breaks my heart I realize that you only want what is best for us, and I am proud of you. You're my husband, my best friend, and I am very proud of you. I know you wanted to be here at the baby's birth, and it breaks my heart that you won't be. But I will be okay, and so will Dakota, we will make sure that the baby knows all about you. . . . We will be here waiting for you to come home. Just be sure you do come home.

At the last line, she held up the letter to shield her welling eyes. On the back of the letter's plastic sleeve, the military stamp glared:

PLEASE BE ADVISED THE CONTENTS MAY CONTAIN HAZARDOUS MATERIAL.

Sergeant Andrew "Andy" Alonzo

Fort Logan National Cemetery, Denver, Colorado

A FRONT-END LOADER BIT into the soft turf at Fort Logan National Cemetery. In one of the city's most peaceful places, the ground rumbled. The caretakers dug the first grave and then started on the second. Andy thought back to the funeral he had attended in Iraq, saluting the empty helmet and combat boots of a fallen friend, forty-one-year-old Staff Sergeant Mark Lawton, who died in an ambush more than a year before.

"You know, I took one of the last pictures of Sergeant Lawton," he said. "It was the day before he was killed. He was sitting under a tree, wearing those big sunglasses of his, reading his Bible."

Andy looked down at another fresh grave. When he returned from Iraq, all of this emotion might have set him off.

"When I first got back, I had the urge to kill somebody," he said quietly. "I was so unhappy with what happened to Sergeant Lawton, but I didn't get to see anybody pay for it. I wanted to kill someone, I wanted to see someone pay."

Back in Andy's hometown, where his family had a bench dedicated to his unit in Iraq, they continued to worry even after his return. Andy never left the house for more than thirty minutes a day. Instead, he holed up, alone, thinking about Iraq, wondering how so many people around him could go on living their lives while the war raged.

"You think, 'Why am I still alive? Why am I so lucky? Why wasn't I on that convoy?' It's always 'What if?' " he said. "In Iraq you would be going down the highway, and you just see an Iraqi body burned up, just out there. People didn't stop to investigate. It was just another body, another casualty of war."

Once he was home, the images followed.

"I did consider suicide," he said. "The closest I had was having the pills out on the counter, ready to take them. But I would always stop myself. I'd stand there, debating whether it was worth it."

At the urging of his family he requested psychological help from the Veterans' Affairs hospital, and the therapy began to help him relax. Then he realized he could also escape to the place he knew best, working out the battlefield in his mind in the place where the battle ultimately ends. In the cemetery he saw young widows and grieving mothers taking care of strangers' graves. He watched as an unborn child—lost to a miscarriage shortly after the baby's father was killed in action—was buried in a grave they had to reopen, so the baby and the soldier could be buried together. At night one of the dead Marines' brothers would sneak in and lie down for hours on the freshly turned soil.

When the war returns to him these days, Andy remembers the face of his fallen sergeant and friend, but he also remembers the faces of children they helped by building schools, and the dead people in the streets. He also remembers a vivid image of a child dancing all alone on the side of a highway.

As his crew prepared the gravesites, Andy headed back to check on the headstones. The sun lowered, painting the graves the color of thunderclouds, stretching their shadows.

"You can't tell people what it's like over there. You can describe it, but you can't feel it," he said and then stopped. "I like to think we did some good over there."

On the morning of the funerals, the Marines arrived early, in formal dress blue uniforms. Andy and his crew arrived even earlier, their shoes dusted with the dirt of new graves. As the body of Lance Corporal Kyle Burns arrived, Andy pulled up with the marble markers.

"I won't leave the stones now," he said.

AFTER THE RIFLE salutes sounded at the funeral shelter nearby, a lieutenant colonel walked up to the mother of Kyle Burns—the same woman who had screamed when she saw the Marines on her snowy porch in Wyoming—and answered some of the questions the family had asked all week.

Yes, it turned out that the two men knew each other, he said. He then told them of that bloody day that would haunt First Lieutenant Webber and the rest of Red Platoon as they continued to fight seven thousand miles away.

As the mourners slowly filed away, Kyle Burns's family remained, waiting to attend the service of Staff Sergeant Holder, the man who had died near their son and whose body would be buried alongside Kyle's.

After the service, Major Beck spoke quietly to a woman propped by a cane and clad in a red wool coat. He gestured toward Jo Burns and told the grieving mother there was someone she should meet—a woman who knew what would come next.

THE FIRST TIME Terry Cooper entered Fort Logan, she sat in the chair up front, the one where nobody ever wants to sit. More than a year earlier, her son, Lance Corporal Thomas Slocum, was the first Coloradan killed in the war with Iraq.

She has attended every service since, often wearing the distinctive red wool coat, and carrying the cane as a result of multiple sclerosis.

Although each funeral saps her, she said she has no choice but to keep coming. Her own son's funeral was a blur, but each time she sees another service, she remembers snippets of the day they buried her Tommy. She also gets a chance to meet the woman she used to be—that grieving mother in the front row, the woman who, since the knock, she will always be.

Terry Cooper isn't the only one who regularly attends the services of men she has never met. Among the crowd at each funeral, alongside veteran Marines in leather jackets and dress blue uniforms, are strangers who never served in the military. Together they form an anonymous fellowship of grief that meets for every active-duty funeral.

"It's like a little family," Mrs. Cooper said of the Marines buried near each other. "They're all there together. I don't want any more members in that family, but I'm glad they're there."

After Kyle Burns's service, at Major Beck's behest, the woman in the red coat walked over to Jo Burns and introduced herself, said she was sorry, and mentioned that Major Beck had told her their sons had a lot in common. After speaking for a few minutes and realizing he was right, she asked a question only a Marine mother would understand: "Was your son as big a little shit as mine?" she asked.

"Yes!" Jo Burns said, exploding with laughter and tears. "Oh, yes!"

MORE THAN AN hour later another funeral procession, carrying the flag-draped casket of Staff Sergeant Sam Holder, wound its way through Fort Logan. There was another rifle salute, another folded flag. When it was all over, a man released doves into the sky.

As the parents of Staff Sergeant Holder left the shelter, Jo and Bob Burns stopped the grieving couple and introduced themselves through tears.

"I'm sorry," Jo Burns said as they embraced.

"I'm sorry," Mary Holder said through more sobs. The Holders finally climbed back into the limousine, promising to keep in touch. Instead of heading back to the car, the Burns family walked to their son's grave.

As they arrived, Andy stood in his cemetery uniform, giving them plenty of space with the stone he had set only minutes before. The family traced the name of their son with their fingers. Then they looked at the open grave only a few yards away.

The family walked off, arm in arm. Andy moved forward, preparing to set the next headstone.

"As I watched [his mother], there were a lot of things going through my mind, but one thing especially," he said. "I wanted to tell her, 'You don't have to worry. We'll take care of him now.' "

12

Jo and Bob Burns

Laramie, Wyoming

THE SOUND OF strapping tape ripped through the living room in Laramie, Wyoming.

"Now for the hard part," Jo Burns said after opening a cardboard box from Iraq filled with her son's possessions. Then she corrected herself. "It's all hard."

It had been more than a month since Major Beck's snowy midnight drive to the white house with the biggest numbers on the block. It had been a couple of weeks since Andrew Alonzo had set their son's stone at Fort Logan. Major Beck wasn't required to personally deliver the boxes to Laramie. He didn't have to stay with the family for two hours more as they sifted through them. Actually, the major said, he had no choice.

"I know that Kyle Burns is looking at me, making sure I'm

squared away—with his family and with him," he said during the drive to Wyoming. "I know I'm going to have to answer the mail on that one day—not with God but with Kyle."

In the living room, near a bare Christmas tree that the family couldn't bring themselves to decorate, Bob Burns began lifting Ziploc bags from the box, cataloging the contents in a shaky voice.

"Here's his wallet," he said as he looked inside. "A fishing license. A hunting license. A Subway Club card? Good grief."

"They're things that reminded him of home," Jo Burns said.

A few minutes later she pulled out a list in her son's handwriting and started to cry.

"What is it, Jo?" Bob Burns asked.

"It's everyone he wanted to call—and write."

"Well," Bob said, "now we have a list, don't we, Jo?"

They found more: a Bible with a splotchy camouflage cover, a giant clothespin, pens with their tops chewed, the government-issued sunglasses he called "military birth control glasses," the keys to his truck, and to the house.

"Shee-sus," Bob Burns said, shaking his head and lifting out a new set of corporal's stripes. "He already bought them," he said. "He only had a couple more tests to take."

Kyle's older brother, Kris, pulled out a book, *Battlefield Okinawa*, feathered the pages, and placed his finger at a wrinkle on the spine.

"Looks like he only got to about here," he said. "He only got halfway through."

He then pulled out one of the tins of Copenhagen his brother was known to hide everywhere. He opened up the tin, took a sniff, and scrunched up his face.

"That's *formaldehagen*," he said, knowing the crack would have made his brother smile: Kyle's favorite joke was "Why was six afraid of seven? Because seven ate nine." When he went out drinking, he wore a cap with rabbit fur ear flaps.

Jo Burns never wanted Kyle to be a Marine. When he invited a recruiter over to meet her, she was openly hostile.

"I have to be honest," she said later. "I didn't believe all that brotherhood bullshit. I thought it was just a bunch of little boys saying things that boys say. I never believed it until after he died."

She whimpered as Major Beck rubbed her back.

"For me, having all this back is a good thing. I want to remember. I don't ever want to forget or to stop feeling. I think Bob feels a little differently."

"I don't want to forget," Kyle's father said. "I just don't want to hurt."

In one of the boxes they found a little snow globe with a typical Wyoming scene: trees, an elk, a bear, and a coyote.

"He said it was so hot over there, he wanted something to remind him of home," Jo Burns said.

She shook the snow globe and watched the flakes fall.

13

Major Steve Beck

Aurora, Colorado

MAJOR BECK LOOKS like the job: hard and soft. His white cotton gloves cover callused hands. They lead to thick, regular guy arms shaped by work instead of weightlifting, and a round, pale face with big cheeks that turn red when he hasn't had enough sleep, which is most of the time. He is as stubborn as he is sensitive, and he is flat-out brash when he needs to be. When working a funeral, he often forgets to eat, fueling himself only with a steady supply of Diet Mountain Dew, which he guzzles by the liter. He can quote war philosophers Carl von Clausewitz and Sun-tzu in regular conversation and will scribble his complex leadership principles and military strategy on cocktail napkins. Still, he never strays far from his roots.

Born in Sand Springs, Oklahoma, he still pronounces his home state "O-koma." He'll describe another Marine's muscles as "hard as a woodpecker's lips," and when he wants something done with precision, he'll require his troops to get it "down to the gnat's ass." The problem is that sometimes, even his friends say, he's the only one who knows where to find the gnat, never mind the ass. He swears he is not a control freak; he says that would imply he wants to tell other people how to think. He says he just knows when things are done properly. He sees his perfectionism as a plus, especially for the delicate duty that involves dealing with people who want everything yesterday and, he believes, deserve it.

"I just don't like to say no," he says of his attempts to grant seemingly impossible requests from grieving families—requests that often go far beyond the requirements of the casualty assistance handbook. After Jo Burns lost her son, she wanted his best friend to be there for the funeral, but the young man's unit was about to deploy to Iraq and was told he couldn't leave. "Roger that," Beck said, and within hours the friend was on his way to Wyoming. He has negotiated with airport officials who initially balked at some families' requests to see their Marine's casket unloaded from the plane, and he has helped track down missing personal items that some families thought were lost forever in Iraq.

Major Beck's car radio is eternally tuned to country music stations. "A day without country music," he insists, "is like a day without sunshine." It's an Everyman quality that can't be faked, one that has become a crucial component in helping the families of fallen Marines.

Although Steve Beck had no training as a casualty assistance officer, in a way he had trained for it all his life. His earliest memory began with a needle. As a toddler he learned to hold a syringe to inject his diabetic mother with insulin. His parents divorced when he was one. Sometimes he was the only one there to help. As he grew up, the family scraped by. Some days he wore Salvation Army clothes to school. Life got harder from there.

When he was thirteen, Steve and his mother watched his three-year-old brother die after being hit by a car. Steve had recently taught the little boy to play catch. Before the funeral he stood at the open casket and placed his brother's baseball glove inside. It took years for the boy and his mother to recover. She retreated and he rebelled, leaving home early. It is a scenario he has seen in the lives of countless other Marines.

"By all accounts," he said, "I should have grown up to be a wife-beating, good-for-nothing troublemaker."

Eventually he channeled his anger into books, even planning to go to medical school, where he hoped to find a cure for his mother's diabetes.

The Persian Gulf War began as he prepared to take his medical school entrance exams. His father had served as a Marine, and Steve had long thought of joining. He figured this would be the war of his generation, and he didn't want to miss it.

"When I first read Sun-tzu, I was like, 'No shit,'" he said of the ancient Chinese strategist who penned *The Art of War*, a text that, in part, details how to win by undermining the enemy. "Honestly, I read that, and it was 'No shit.' I grew up fighting like that."

His mother died while he was attending officer training school.

When he lost her, he also lost his reason for studying medicine. He never went back. Although he had grown up distanced from his father, a cop and former Drug Enforcement Administration agent, they eventually reconciled. Then his father was diagnosed with cancer.

"On my last trip out to see him, I took a drive with him and asked him if there was anything I could do," Major Beck said. "He asked me if I could get a color guard at his funeral," he said, referring to the formally dressed Marines who perform the flag-folding ceremony. "That's all he asked for, a Marine color guard. I said, 'Dad, that's easy.'

"I didn't get to talk to him again."

14

Melissa, Dakota, and Carson Givens

Fountain, Colorado

I N THE SPRING of 2004, yellow ribbons and WELCOME banners dangled from thousands of houses near the Fort Carson Army post as soldiers arrived home from their first tour. Two doors down from Melissa Givens's house, one soldier stood in his driveway, fixing his motorcycle, still dressed in fatigues.

"I realized I can't avoid it," Melissa said. "I was going to go home [to Missouri] this month, but I changed my mind. I'm going to have to get used to it. All these guys coming home this month, that's going to hurt like hell."

Still, instead of averting her eyes, she tried to find a schedule that kept her busy. Along with Dakota's school, his karate classes, and Carson's feedings, her new definition of a *normal* routine included regular meetings with a group of widows, few of them older than thirty.

Thanks to Jesse's life insurance and the military death benefits, Melissa figured she could concentrate on Carson and Dakota instead of having to find a job. It was an enormous relief, she said, since the busiest part of her day often came in the middle of the night.

"Sometimes I'll find Dakota crying in a corner downstairs, still asleep," she said. "I'll find him in different places all over the house, crying. Those are the scariest nights."

Then there are her own nightmares. After midnight she sometimes finds herself in the basement, avoiding the dreams by scribbling in her journal. On other nights, she will spend hours writing to friends, and sometimes even strangers online.

Nine months after her husband's death, she logged on to a Web site called fallenheroesmemorial.com, where people from around the nation have posted tributes to her husband. Alone in the basement that night, she began to type:

> *Jesse, hey baby. . . . Just when I think it's going to get a little better it starts to hurt so bad again. . . . Dakota and I talk about heaven and I tell him you are there waiting for us, he wanted you to ask God that when he gets to go there if he can be a little boy again so you can give him piggy back rides. He also asked if they have parks there so the two of you can play. He told me that he was sorry he wasn't being good the last time you took him to the park. I tell him it's ok and you understand and he can tell you*

when he gets there.... Through my tears I can't see to type anymore....

WHEN DEPLOYMENT DAY finally arrived on April 6, 2003, Melissa and Dakota felt as if they were the ones leaving. Neither said good-bye.

Melissa was sick, seven months pregnant, and overwhelmed with tears. Dakota went to play with the other children at the post. Melissa kept crying.

After waiting several hours for the bus to come and take her husband away, Melissa finally decided she couldn't take the stress. After midnight she put Dakota in the car and drove home.

"The last thing I remember is looking in the rearview mirror and him standing in the parking lot, crying," Melissa said. "Since then I've thought, 'Should I have stayed for those extra couple of minutes?' I've felt a lot of guilt about that. For not staying as long as I could have. We've never been good at saying good-bye. The only other time he really left was when I dropped him off at the bus station once when he went back to see his mom. I dropped him off at the bus station and just drove away. I'm really good at just driving away."

While Dakota played with a stack of LEGO blocks nearby, the little boy listened to his mother talk, reminded of the last day he saw his father. "And I didn't really say 'bye to him," the six-year-old said, his eyes wide. "I just wanted to play."

"I know," his mother said, "but that's okay, Dakota. He understood that you wanted to play with the other kids. And I know that you now kinda feel bad, that you wish you'd stayed with him more. But he understands that. And when you get to heaven, you'll get to hang out with him then."

"But how will I find him?" Dakota asked. "It's a big place."

"I think you just know," his mother said.

I have never been so blessed as the day I met Melissa. You are my angel, soul mate, wife, lover, and my best friend. I am sorry. I did not want to have to write this letter. There is so much more I need to say, so much more I need to share. A million lifetimes' worth. I married you for a million lifetimes. That's how long I will be with you. Please keep our babies safe. Please find it in your heart to forgive me for leaving you alone. . . . Do me a favor, after you tuck Toad and Bean in, give them hugs and kisses from me. Go outside, look at the stars and count them. Don't forget to smile.

Love Always
Your husband
Jess

In the living room, Melissa looked up toward the high window where the American flag from Jesse's casket is folded into a tight triangle so that only the white stars are visible. Beyond them, outside, the sky was dark.

"If you lay on that couch on a clear night," she said, "you can see the stars perfectly."

. . .

ON THE NIGHT before what would have been Jesse's thirty-fifth birthday, Melissa and Dakota walked to the boy's bedroom carrying a videotape of Jesse reading traditional good-night stories, and a secret message of his own.

Underneath another portrait of Jesse that dominates the room, Melissa walked to the VCR near the boy's television set and pushed PLAY.

On the screen, Jesse appeared on the couch, looking exhausted, holding a book called *What Daddies Can't Do* as he sat alongside Dakota. The date flashed in the corner of the screen—April 5, 2003—his last night at home.

Jesse read *The Lorax* and *The Very Hungry Caterpillar*. Then he turned to the boy on the couch. "You know why we're making this?" he asked.

"So you can read me books?" Dakota said.

"While I'm gone . . . so I can read you books when I'm gone, and you can see me, and it'll be sorta like I'm here—sorta, but not really."

After he finished reading, the screen went blank, and then Jesse reappeared, in a scene he secretly recorded only hours before he left.

Okay, you guys. We did the stories. Now I want to take some time by myself to tell you I love you very much. Melissa, please take care of Dakota and give him hugs and kisses. Dakota, please take care of your mom. When the Bean gets here, tell him I love him very much. Sorry I wasn't here. Give him hugs and kisses for me. Say your prayers every night.

I'm with you all the time. My heart's with you; my mind's with you; my soul's with you. You're my family. You've made me happier than I could ever be, and I'll be home as soon as I can.

Dakota, don't let the fuzzy butt-tickling monkey get you or the toe-eating alligator. Um, I'm not real good at this kind of stuff. Buddy, I'm proud of you. You're the most wonderful boy a guy could have, and I'm going to miss you a lot.

Melissa, I'm sorry I'm not going to be home. I'm sorry. Sometimes it doesn't seem like I do everything I can, but I do the best I can.

I love you guys. I'm going to miss you with all my heart, and I'll be thinking about you all the time. I'll be praying for you. I'll be home as soon as I can. I love you guys.

"Wait!" shouted Dakota as the screen went black again and Melissa moved to push Stop.

"Wait!" he said.

"I want to kiss Daddy."

Melissa, frozen for a second, wiped her eyes, rewound the tape, and watched as the little boy leaped from his bed.

As the end of the tape played again, Dakota walked to the television and pressed his lips to the screen on the image of his father's face. Then he looked back and found the words they all forgot to say:

"Bye-bye, Daddy."

15

Marine Air Control Squadron 23

Buckley Air Force Base, Aurora, Colorado

BEFORE GRADUATING FROM boot camp, every Marine masters the blank stare: the focused but distant look that glares down from recruiting posters, the one meant to strike fear in enemies, the one intended to convey more than two centuries of tradition.

Marines are taught to hold the stare no matter the distraction. If a fly crawls on their face or in their ear, they are ordered to remain steady. But no training could prepare them for the funerals.

According to protocol—an extension of their sacred "Never leave a Marine behind" mandate—a fallen Marine's body must be guarded whenever it is accessible by a member of the public. While they trained for war, the active-duty Marines stationed at Buckley Air Force Base took turns standing guard over the caskets. Inevitably, they learned about the life of the person inside. Underneath the formal white caps they call "covers," many of the Buckley Marines keep the funeral brochures of every Marine they have watched over.

"Now they're watching over us," Sergeant Andrea Fitzgerald said as she turned over her cap, revealing a photo tucked inside. "I call them my angels."

During visitations Marines hear the families talk to the body. At the memorial services they listen to the eulogies. During the burials they see the flag presented to the grieving mother or widow.

Through it all they try to hold the stare. They can stand still for hours. Their feet fall asleep up to their knees.

"The pain we're feeling drives us. It drives us for the family because the pride is bigger than the pain," Major Beck said. "But the pain—you gotta eat it, you gotta live with it, you gotta take it home and cry in the dark. What else are you going to do?"

For Staff Sergeant Kevin Thomas it starts when the Marines first meet the casket at the airport.

"You always hear all these statements like 'Freedom isn't free.' You hear the president talking about all these people making sacrifices," he said. "But you never really know until you carry one of them in the casket. When you feel their body weight, when you feel them, that's when you know. That's when you understand."

Staff Sergeant Thomas said he would rather be in Iraq or any place he doesn't feel so helpless. Still, he said, he has learned lessons from funeral duty that he knows combat can't teach.

"I'll be sitting in front of the computer, and I'll see the news:

Another service member killed. It's enough to choke me up, tighten my chest. That's another hundred people that are about to be affected," Staff Sergeant Thomas said. "All these things their parents are going to miss—watching their son get married, have children, watching their parents become grandparents. It makes you forget everything that's important—well, everything that society makes you want to think is important. There's no way that doing one of these funerals can't make you a better person. I think everyone in the military should have to do at least one."

Some of Staff Sergeant Thomas's friends had been deployed twice already, but he had yet to be sent to Iraq. As much as the Marines will say they train so they never have to fight, once the battle begins, they want to be in the middle of it. Imagine training for your whole life to be a lawyer, one said, and never entering a courtroom. Imagine training for years as a journalist and never writing a story.

"It makes me feel guilty. People come up to me and say, 'Thank you for serving our country.' I want to say, 'I haven't done shit.' I want to take the Global War on Terrorism medal home and give it to my son," he said. "He's done as much as I have."

Staff Sergeant Thomas couldn't name many of the Marines he has been stationed with for three years. He never forgets the name of someone he has helped bury.

"Sometimes I'll just be sitting out on the back porch, drinking a beer, and I'll start thinking about it. It's those times, when you're doing the regular things that people do—sitting outside on the back porch drinking a beer—and I'll think, 'He's never going to do this.' "

Then, inevitably, the burden returns.

"I agree with what we're doing [in Iraq], but the funerals, they exhaust you. It's not the physical part. It's just so exhausting. It makes me feel guilty for saying that. I feel a sense of loss even though I didn't know the person. But the family members come up, and they speak to you, and there's nothing you can say. Often it's just a handshake. The standard line is 'It's an honor and a privilege to do this.' But that feels so inadequate. You want to do so much for them, and you just don't know what to do. There's no way to convey it. There are no words in the English language. . . . I'll go off for a walk, have a cigarette . . . to keep from crying like a baby."

16

Major Steve Beck

Denver, Colorado

S HE SAT in his truck outside another funeral home, Major Beck rubbed his temples with his thumb and forefinger.

"I've never really had a headache like the ones I've been getting lately. It's not really a headache as much as—I don't know. Just reaching my max."

He had walked the same tightrope since his first notification. He had seen the job drain some of his best men and women.

"There are a couple Marines I'm going to send off for a while. I know what it's doing to me, and I'm starting to see it in them," he said. "There are also Marines who I may not put up to this yet—Marines who I don't think are ready for that flood."

Although he said he felt the effects of the notifications, both physical and mental, he rarely acknowledged them to anyone but himself. Still, at one point even his superior officers said they saw the toll of the assignment on Major Beck.

"There were times that he was absolutely exhausted, and I was worried about him. And I didn't know when he was sleeping. I asked him if he needed support," said Colonel Ben Stein, who helped oversee the Marines at Major Beck's base. "I told him, 'Nobody is going to make that call for you.' He kept saying, 'As long as my family supports me, I'll be okay.'"

After the viewing at the funeral home, as Major Beck drove away, he remained focused on the image of the dead Marine's mother in the front pew.

"That mother, I would suck all her pain away if I could," he said. "Every Marine would. They'd take every ounce of pain and just absorb it."

Inside his truck, Major Beck began to cry. "It bubbles up," he said later. "Yeah, it bubbles up, but God helps me with it."

Ingrained in his faith, Major Beck said, is a strength he takes from every Marine whose funeral he oversees. Although other notification officers compare the aftereffects of the knock to the front lines of the battlefield, Major Beck immediately shakes off any comparison.

"You think about what those Marines did and what I did. Can you possibly find the balance? It's not even close," he said. "They carry me. We may carry them, but they certainly carry us."

PART 3

BRINGING THEM HOME

I'm just chilled that that body is on here.

—MICHAEL LIPKIN

17

Navy Corpsman HM3 Christopher "Doc" Anderson

Philadelphia, Pennsylvania

 SKINNY SAILOR SAT in the Philadelphia airport terminal in his Navy blue dress uniform, cracking his knuckles, shifting in his seat, waiting for his best friend.

A woman from the airline walked over and motioned for him to follow. She saw the nervous look on the sailor's face and stopped.

"Wait," she said. "Is this your first time doing this?"

"Yes, ma'am," the twenty-two-year-old said, his voice cracking.

"Well, unfortunately, it's not the first time for me," she said. "Not even the first time this week."

She led him toward the gate and gave him a soft smile. "You'll do fine," she said.

Inside the airport, the public-address system pumped out Brenda Lee's "Rockin' Around the Christmas Tree." A nearby group of passengers loaded up their ski clothes, readying for a vacation. Suit-and-tied businessmen with premier privileges watched as the sailor was led to the front of them all.

Aboard the nearly empty plane a flight attendant was one of the first to shake his hand.

"I understand you're escorting today," he said. "I'm sure you'll do yourself and your service proud."

After speaking with the crew, the pilot walked over and offered his hand.

"I understand he was your friend," the captain said. "I'm sorry."

The sailor nodded. He carried his soft white hat in his hands. The winding snake patch on his left shoulder signified his status as a Navy hospital corpsman. The captain then looked at one of the crew members.

"Are there any seats in first class? I'd like to bring him up here."

After the sailor stowed his bags, the woman from the terminal walked him back out to the Jetway, where he waited as the other passengers boarded the plane. As they filed past, some stole glances at him. Some smiled at him. He tried to smile back.

Another flight attendant, a Vietnam veteran, walked over.

"Hello," he said, grasping the sailor's hand. "Thirty years ago they didn't say thank-you to us. I wanted to say thank-you now."

The sailor nodded again and managed a grin. Then the chief of the ground crew opened the door to the stairs that led to the tarmac.

"Okay," he said. "We're ready."

· · ·

UNDERNEATH A DRONING jet engine near the rear cargo hold, baggage workers lifted the tarp on a cart. Hospital Corpsman Third Class John Dragneff swallowed hard. The skinny sailor checked to see if the name on the cardboard box printed with an American flag matched the name of his best friend.

The cardboard encased the polished hardwood casket, protecting it during transit from Dover Air Force Base to the airport and then to Denver, where the box would be removed before anyone saw it. The box was stamped on each end with a large official seal of the Department of Defense.

The last time John saw his friend was the same day Christopher "Doc" Anderson left for Iraq. They talked endlessly that day, about taking care of each other's families, about taking care in general. That was, after all, what they had in common.

Often in restaurants the waitperson would ask the sailors, "Are you brothers?" The first few times they laughed it off. After a while they started answering without hesitation, "Yes."

The two young men had met at field medical training school and clicked. They soon studied together, relaxed at the beach together, and just generally hung out, talking about where life was headed for both of them. More recently, they spent time talking about what it meant to hold somebody's life in your hands—and to lose it.

Then the young sailor stood on the chilly tarmac in Philadelphia. As the casket ascended the conveyor belt, he snapped to attention, grasping his hands into fists, thumbs at the seams of his pants, trying to squeeze back the tears.

His eyes emptied as he brought his hand to his face in a salute, which he tried to hold steady until the casket disappeared into the plane's belly.

He turned and walked into the embrace of Pamela Andrus, the United Airlines service director. The ground manager took his other side, supporting him.

"I'm so sorry," she said.

Together they walked back up the stairs and into the plane, where a cheery flight attendant came over with several tissues plucked from the lavatory.

"You can cry," Christine Sullivan told him. "All of us want to send our love and blessings to you and be here for you. You're going to do great."

I N THE FIRST-CLASS section of United Airlines Flight 271 from Philadelphia to Denver, John looked through a booklet called *Manual for Escorts of Deceased Naval Personnel*.

"It's weird. I think back, and I was never an emotional-type person until I joined the military," he said. "In the past I've had relatives who died, but I never really cried. I guess that since I've been in, it all means a lot more."

He thought back to one of the last times he saw Chris—long

before his best friend had earned the nickname Doc. They had visited Arlington National Cemetery on Memorial Day, and John found the grave of a fellow sailor he barely knew.

"When we went out to Arlington, standing there, I just started crying, and I couldn't understand why. I didn't really know the guy that well," he said. "Chris just grabbed me and hugged me and let me sit there and cry. As we were walking away, a man walked up and shook my hand and said, 'Thank you.' So then Chris started to cry. So there were just the three of us standing there, crying. A few minutes later, just trying to cheer me up, he made up some story about a squirrel on crack. Just like that. He could make you smile."

John was the responsible one, relatively shy, the designated driver who didn't drink or smoke. He was the one happy in a sweatshirt and jeans, while Chris would change clothes five times before going out wearing Armani or Ralph Lauren. At six-foot-two, with short-cropped black hair and hazel eyes, the muscular, outgoing twenty-four-year-old never lacked self-confidence.

"Damn, I look good," he wrote on one of the photos displayed on his myspace.com account. John posted regular updates on the Web site about his friend while Doc was in Iraq. He was also the one to inform its readers of Chris's death.

Dec 5 2006 12:56P

Christopher Anderson, you weren't a "real" brother, but you were still my brother. A person could not ask for a better friend or brother. You will be greatly missed. Love your brother, John.

Rest in peace.

. . .

CHRISTOPHER ANDERSON ENLISTED in the Navy in 2005, just as men in his family had for the past three generations. At boot camp he was voted the honor graduate in his class. After that he wanted to excel in everything.

Before he left for Iraq, Christopher and his father visited military supply shops looking for equipment that might help him in the field. He wanted to blend in with the Marines since he knew corpsmen were prime targets.

"I have to be able to do this in the dark," he told his father.

In Iraq he asked to be stationed with the frontline Marines and was assigned to a twelve-man unit. One of his first tasks was to memorize each Marine's medical records.

Christopher's calls from Iraq usually came at about 5:00 A.M., so Rick and Debra Anderson put the phone between them in bed and listened.

"One time . . . my wife heard some funny noises and heard shouts of 'Where's that coming from? Where's that coming from?'" Rick Anderson remembered.

"I'm going to stay down here," Christopher told them. "I'll just belly-crawl down the hallway so I can talk to you."

During one mortar attack, a shell barely missed him. The blast lifted him into the air and threw him to the ground, but he survived with only serious bruises. Later, after another attack, he crouched in the back of a Humvee, his hands covered with his sergeant's blood, speeding toward a field hospital, tying tourniquets and offering encouragement.

Before he left for Iraq, Christopher and his father talked about the possibility that he wouldn't return, and Christopher asked for a burial at Arlington. He had only one other request: "If something happens," he told his father, "I want John there."

A T 31,000 FEET, word slipped through the plane about the sailor in first class and his mission.

When the passengers found out, their emotions spanned the debate that continued to split the country. Some cursed President George W. Bush by name. Others cursed anyone who said they support the troops without supporting the war. Despite their political leanings, they all voiced appreciation for the sailor in the front of the plane—whom most of them called "the kid"—and, even more, the one in the cargo hold beneath them.

Seat 33F, Patrick Mondile, Philadelphia:

"I look at my own situation—I'm twenty-four years old. I think [that] it very well could have been me if I'd chosen that path. I have friends over there right now," Mondile said. "I don't understand why we're there [in Iraq], but I feel for the families—not just for this soldier but the thousands who have died."

Seat 14A, Pam Anderson, New Jersey:

"God bless him. God bless him," the sixty-two-year-old said of the sailor in first class. "If he wants any free hugs, just send him back here. I'm serious. I'm completely serious. I joined the Air Force as a flight nurse, and my squadron is taking a lot of men and women out of the field right now."

Seats 8D, 8E, Dave and Lindy Powell, Monument, Colorado:

"To me it's a sense of honor. We didn't know him, but he's part of the Colorado family. We're from Monument, so he's part of our family, too," Dave Powell said.

"Our nephew is a C-130 pilot who's flying into Iraq and Afghanistan. Kids in my Scout troop joined the Marines and went right to Baghdad."

His voice broke.

"They all came home safely."

Seat 22D, Terry Musgrove, Ontario, Oregon:

"If we don't support them, then it's going to embolden the terrorists," he said, fuming as he spoke about a new poll indicating declining support for the war. Before the flight took off, he was the only passenger to shake the skinny sailor's hand at the terminal.

"It breaks my heart to know that he's on the plane. I had no idea," he said as he began to cry. "But I'm proud to tell you I'm proud."

Seat 16F, Michael Lipkin, Aspen, Colorado:

"I think it's extremely sobering. This is a war where few of us have family and friends over there, and despite the fact that it dominates the media, I think most of us don't feel the cost, the real cost of this war. And we're going to be paying it for a long time," Lipkin said. "I'm just chilled that that body is on here."

18

Major Steve Beck

Aurora, Colorado

THE BOOKSHELF IN Major Beck's home office is packed with titles such as *On Killing, Islam in Focus, The Peloponnesian War*, and *The 9/11 Commission Report*. His copy of Clausewitz's *On War* is dog-eared and highlighted.

Outside his house, he grows his own camouflage.

"I challenge you to find snapdragons growing anywhere else right now," he said as he showed off the flowers. "And look at this wisteria. Have you ever seen wisteria bloom? I spend at least five minutes out here each day. I try to spend a lot more. I just like color. I spent three years in Twentynine Palms [California] in the high desert, where there's nothing but snakes and lizards—and Marines. I just like color. Plus, it's a little mindless.

"You don't have to write that down," he added. "You're going to emasculate the Marine Corps."

At the time, Beck was squabbling with his superiors over the costs associated with the way he cared for the families. The price of bringing his Marines to several states, housing them in hotels, and continuing to follow up with the families had broken his budget, which was earmarked for war training only. Beck argued that the added cost should have come directly from the Department of Defense. He refused to stop spending money on the families.

"I figured if we're spending GWOT (Global War on Terrorism) money to send our Marines over there, and GWOT money to equip them and pay them while they're there, why shouldn't we be using GWOT money to bring them home with the honor they deserve? . . . I call it the inertia and momentum of noble acts. The ball's moving, and it's speeding up. Get on or get out of the way."

In his home office where the bookshelves were filled with tales of war and peace, he opened another book that is just as well worn as *On War*: his copy of the Bible, the book he says he retreats to more than any other. Although at times he can swear and growl like only a Marine can, he says his prayers are just as fierce. His faith, he says, has only been strengthened by the knock.

"One of the things I've learned from all this," he said, "[is that] there's a difference between believing and knowing. Before, there were some things I believed. Now, I know."

When Major Beck and his wife, Julie, first moved to Colorado with three young children in early 2004, they were told the assignment was likely a "family tour," with time to reconnect after being stationed in several states. After more than fifteen years of marriage, Julie Beck looked forward to building the new family and a new life.

Before her husband's first casualty call, she worried about the things that most new mothers and transplants worry about: daily stresses dealing with the house and the kids while her husband spent eighty-hour weeks learning the intricacies of the new job. She wondered when *she* would get a break. Then the call came.

"When the first casualty happened, it was a wake-up call that 'it's not about me. This chapter is not about me at all,'" Julie said. "Thinking about these families losing their sons hit so hard and forced me to step out of my little fishbowl. . . . When Steve would come home from a notification, he was here. He gets to have another day. These boys don't get another day. We do. And we have to use them."

Although she has a degree in psychology, Julie said she didn't try to analyze her husband. Instead, she waited for him to open up, and meanwhile she held down the home, allowing him to care for the families of strangers. When the calls came in the middle of the night, she awoke alongside her husband. As he organized the logistics from his cell phone, she would quietly gather his uniform. After he left for the notifications, she would not fall back to sleep. Instead, she imagined her husband on the porch.

"In that one second I felt so bad for him. I obviously felt bad for the families, but I also felt sad for him," she said. "He was the one standing there. My heart ached for him."

One night in a hotel room after a memorial service, Major Beck opened his computer and began typing. He wrote letters, addressed them to Julie and his children, and included detailed instructions that he hoped would remain unread for decades. He stored the file on his computer and called it "In case of my death."

"My wife hasn't read it, but she knows it's there," he said. "I want them to know how much they mean."

Still, he has his secrets: the tear-streaked drives home he has never discussed with Julie and the dark moments he shared only in his prayers.

"Don't put in that stuff I said about my flowers," he said firmly. "I'm serious. Don't you dare put that in there."

19

Marine Second Lieutenant
James J. Cathey

Reno, Nevada

INSIDE A LIMOUSINE parked on the airport tarmac, Katherine Cathey looked out at the clear night sky and felt a kick.

"He's moving," she said. "Come feel him. He's moving."

Her two best friends leaned forward on the soft leather seats and put their hands on her stomach.

"I felt it," one of them said. "I felt it."

Outside, the whine of jet engines swelled.

"Oh, sweetie," her friend said. "I think this is his plane."

As the three young women peered through the tinted windows, Katherine squeezed a set of dog tags stamped with the same name as her unborn son: James J. Cathey.

"He wasn't supposed to come home this way," she said, tightening her grip on the tags that were linked by a necklace to her husband's wedding ring.

The women looked through the back window. Then the twenty-three-year-old placed her hand on her pregnant belly.

"Everything that made me happy is on that plane," she said.

They watched as airport workers rolled a conveyor belt to the rear of the plane, followed by six solemn Marines.

Katherine turned from the window and closed her eyes.

"I don't want it to be dark right now. I wish it was daytime," she said. "I wish it was daytime for the rest of my life. The night is just too hard."

Suddenly, the car door opened. A white-gloved hand reached into the limousine from outside. It was the same hand that knocked on Katherine's door in Colorado five days earlier.

The man in the deep blue uniform knelt down to meet her eyes, speaking in a soft, steady voice.

"Katherine," said Major Beck, "it's time."

THE AMERICAN AIRLINES 757 couldn't have landed much farther from the war.

The plane arrived in Reno on a Friday evening, the beginning of the 2005 "Hot August Nights" festival—one of the city's biggest—filled with flashing lights, fireworks, car shows, and plenty of gambling.

When a young Marine in dress uniform boarded the plane to Reno, the passengers smiled and nodded politely. On the flight the woman sitting next to him nodded toward his uniform and asked if he was coming or going. To the war, she meant.

He fell back on the words the military had told him to say: "I'm escorting a fallen Marine home to his family from the situation in Iraq."

The woman quietly said she was sorry. Then she began to cry.

When the plane landed in Nevada, the sergeant was allowed to disembark alone. Outside, a procession walked toward the cargo hold. The airline passengers pressed their faces against the windows.

From their seats in the plane they saw a hearse and a Marine extending a white-gloved hand into a limousine. In the plane's cargo hold, Marines readied the flag-draped casket and placed it on the luggage conveyor belt.

Inside the plane, the passengers couldn't hear the screams.

A T THE SIGHT of her husband's casket, Katherine let loose a shrill, full-body wail that gave way to moans of distilled contagious grief.

She screamed as the casket moved slowly down the conveyor belt. She screamed until she nearly collapsed, clutching Major Beck around the neck.

When the pallbearers lifted the casket, they struggled visibly with the weight, their eyes filling with tears as they shuffled to the white hearse.

Of all the Marines they had met or trained with, Jim Cathey was the one they considered invincible—a kid who had made sergeant at nineteen and seemed destined to leapfrog through the ranks.

Most of the Marines who would serve as pallbearers had first met "Cat" at the University of Colorado while enrolled in an elite scholarship program for enlisted Marines taking the difficult path to becoming officers. They partied with him, occasionally got into trouble with him, and then watched him graduate in only three years with honors in anthropology and history.

After they placed the casket inside the hearse, Katherine fell onto one corner, pressing her face into the blue field of stars.

Major Beck put a hand on her back as she held the casket tight. By then he knew her well enough to understand that she wouldn't let go. He kept his hand on her back until he found a solution.

"Would you like to ride with him?" he finally asked. She looked up, dazed, and replied with a sniffling nod. She took his hand again as he guided her to the front seat of the hearse, where the surprised funeral directors quickly moved papers to make room for her.

Jim Cathey's mother, father, and sister took their own time with the casket, caressing the flag.

His mother, Caroline, thought of the baby who used to reach out to her from the crib. His father, Jeff, saw the boy he watched grow into a man on long hunting trips through the barren landscape.

His sister, Joyce, saw the kid who became her protector. The day after she learned of his death, she had the image of his face tattooed on the back of her neck. That way, she said, he would always be watching her back.

Last of all, the young Marine who had escorted his friend home walked up to the casket and came to attention.

A year earlier Gavin Conley had stood before his best friend at the formal commissioning ceremony in Colorado, where Jim received his brass lieutenant's bars. It was one of the most important days of Jim's life, and Gavin knew the best way to share his pride. He walked up to the new lieutenant and snapped his arm to his brow, giving the new officer his first salute.

In front of the casket on the tarmac, Gavin again brought his hand to his face, this time in one slow, sweeping movement. As the family wept, his hand fell to his side.

Before climbing into the hearse with Katherine, Major Beck took one last look toward the plane. By then the passengers had moved on, leaving the Marines and the family alone with the casket and everything that was about to follow.

W HEN JIM AND Katherine met, he didn't need an opening line. "Hi, I'm Cat," he said.

"Hey, I'm Kat, too," said the woman who in just four months would become Katherine Cathey.

They married at the justice of the peace in Denver, expecting to hold a formal wedding once he returned from Iraq.

Although he stood more than six feet tall and had steel-cable arms and shoulders covered in tattoos—a guy whom even burly bouncers in bars would shy away from—"Cat" also wielded a disarming charm and tenderness that were hidden in the bulk.

Jim Cathey could knit and cross-stitch, and was a master at sewing. He was just as proficient at hunting birds and was well known for his penchant for fun—including his ability to knock back Jägermeister shots and his tendency to transform a karaoke microphone into an amplified outlet for bodily noises and bathroom humor.

Even then he knew when the fun stopped.

"One time we were leaving a bar, and there was a woman who was staggering around the parking lot, about to get in her car and drive home. We'd seen her drinking in the bar all night," said Sean McDonald, his brother-in-law. "He went up to her and told her she shouldn't be driving. Then he saw the [military identification] on the car and asked, 'Is your husband in the military?' She said, 'Yes, he's in Iraq.'

"He said, 'That's every Marine's worst nightmare, thinking that his wife will be killed while he's in the field.' Then Jim made sure she got a cab. Everyone else was just walking their separate ways. He cared."

The day Jim left for Iraq, Kat and Cat said good-bye seven times.

"There were all these delays, and each time he would run off the bus and grab me," she said. "We kept thinking it was going to be our final good-bye, and then we'd get another chance."

Before he left, he gave her his wedding ring, which he couldn't wear in the field. In its place he had her name tattooed around his ring finger.

On the day he deployed, he handed her one more note.

I have been pondering for the past three hours over what I should write in this card. However, the only things I have come to realize is how there are no words to describe how much I love you, and will miss you. I will also promise you one thing: I will be home. I have a wife and a new baby to take care of, and you guys are my world.

THE FLAG NEVER left Jim Cathey. As his body was flown from Iraq, the sturdy, heavyweight cotton flag remained nearby, following him from the desert to Dover Air Force Base, Delaware, where a mortuary affairs team received his body.

Members of Second Lieutenant Cathey's unit told family members that he was leading the search of an abandoned building when a booby-trapped door exploded. The explosion was so fierce that it blew an arm and a leg off the Marine directly behind Cathey, but that Marine somehow survived.

Once Jim Cathey's remains arrived at Dover, the mortuary affairs team began the delicate task of readying his body for the final trip home. Specialists wrapped his body in a white shroud and covered it with a satin body-length pillow and his dress blue uniform before closing the casket lid.

When the plane landed in Reno, the casket was loaded into the hearse to continue its journey to the funeral home. After all the noise at the airport—the screaming, the crying, the whining of jet engines—the funeral home was quiet enough to hear each footstep, even on the carpet.

The pallbearers carried their friend's body to the front of a gaping empty room and then faded into the background. Major Beck posted himself at the head of the casket, his face frozen in the Marine stare.

With his eyes trained forward, he still saw everything. In the room Caroline Cathey bent down to hug Katherine. They squeezed each other for a long time.

"You give me strength," the young widow said.

Other family members sat on couches and the floor, hugging and holding hands, with their eyes locked on the casket for nearly half an hour. Major Beck finally broke the silence.

"I'm sorry," he said, asking the family to leave the room. "There are some things I need to do."

MAJOR BECK MOTIONED to the pallbearers and began the instructions that would hold for the next three days. Although the Marines are required to stand watch over a comrade's body, they usually leave at night once the casket is safely inside a locked mortuary or church and return when the mortuary reopens.

This time, however, the watch would not end.

"Katherine and Caroline have both expressed concerns about Jim's being left alone," Major Beck told the Marines. "So we won't leave him alone."

He then explained how to guard the casket. They all had posted watch before. They had stood at attention for hours as part of basic training—one of them had even stood guard at the White House—but it was nothing like this. Major Beck told them to take shifts of about an hour at a time and stand watch twenty-four hours a day. When changing the guard, they were to salute Jim's casket first and then relieve the other Marine the same way. He showed them the slow salute that isn't taught in basic training: three seconds up, hold for three seconds, and three seconds down.

"A salute to your fallen comrade should take time," he said.

For Major Beck that salute embodied more than the movement itself. Earlier in the day, someone had asked him about the arrival of "the body." He held up his hand with a firm correction.

" 'The body' has a name," he said. "His name is Jim."

In the room he walked up to the casket and paused.

"Now, this is important, too," he said. "If a family member wants you to break, you can break. They may want to hug you or kiss you. That's okay. Hug them. If someone wants to shake your hand, shake their hand. I'll take my glove off when I shake their hand—you don't have to, it's up to you. But then go back to position. Everyone understand?"

"Yes, sir," they responded. "Roger that."

"This is a serious business," he said. "Jim is watching you."

As the other Marines filed into the hallway, closing the door behind them, Major Beck walked back to the casket. For the first time he and Jim Cathey were alone. It was time for the final inspection.

· · ·

Major Beck walked up to the casket and lifted the flag, tucking it into neat pleats and leaving just enough room to open the heavy wooden lid. He walked around the casket several times, making sure each stripe lined up straight, smoothing the thick stitching with his soft white gloves.

Then he lifted the lid.

For the past five days Major Beck had spent hours looking at pictures of Jim Cathey, listening to the family's stories, and dabbing their tears. When he looked inside, they were no longer strangers.

For the next ten minutes Major Beck leaned over the open casket, checking the empty uniform that lay atop the tightly shrouded body, making sure every ribbon and medal was in place. Occasionally, he pulled off a piece of lint or a stray thread and flicked it away.

Although casualty assistance officers receive an advisory from military morticians about whether a body is "viewable," some families insist on looking. The casualty assistance officer is often the one to make last-minute recommendations, since by then he or she knows the family and—after the final inspection—knows exactly what the family will see.

Whether or not the family decides on a viewing, Major Beck said, the procedure is no less meticulous.

Jim Cathey's survivors decided not to look under the shroud.

But Katherine wanted a few minutes alone with the open casket, to give her husband a few of the things they had shared—and one he never got to see.

Major Beck ran his hand alongside the shroud, taking one last look at the uniform. He then closed the lid and turned toward the door.

KATHERINE PRESSED HER pregnant belly to the casket, as close to a hug as she could get.

Major Beck placed a hand on her back.

"Tell me when you're ready," he said. "Take your time."

He stepped back.

The air conditioner clicked on, filling the room with a low hum. Ten minutes passed. It clicked off, leaving the room to her soft moans.

Katherine closed her eyes and whispered something.

Then she looked up at Major Beck.

"Okay," she said.

As she stood at his arm, he opened the casket.

She did not cry. She did not speak. He gave her a few seconds and then took her hand and brought it to the middle of the empty uniform. He held her hand there and pressed down.

"He's here," he told her. "Feel right here."

She held her hand on the spot, pressing the uniform into the shrouded body beneath. She dragged her hand the length of all that was there.

Major Beck walked back to get the personal belongings Katherine had brought with her from Colorado.

"Where do you want to start?" he asked.

"With the picture of us kissing," she said.

She placed the picture at the top of the casket, above the neck of the uniform. She bent down and pressed her lips to it.

"I'm always kissing you, baby," she whispered.

She took several other photos of their lives together and placed them around the uniform. She gently added a bottle of her perfume and then picked up the dried fragile flowers of her wedding bouquet. Her wedding dress still hung in her closet at home, unworn.

She placed the flowers alongside the uniform and then turned again to the major.

"The ultrasound," she said.

The fuzzy image was taken two days after her husband's death. Katherine had scheduled the appointment for a day when Jim was supposed to call so they could both learn the baby's gender together. He had a feeling it was a boy, he had told her. If it was, she suggested they name the child after him.

She stood cradling the ultrasound image and then moved forward and placed it on the pillow at the head of the casket. She stood there, watching for several minutes, and then removed it.

She walked the length of the casket and then stepped back, still holding the only image of James J. Cathey Jr.

She leaned in and placed it over her husband's heart.

20

Navy Corpsman HM3 Christopher "Doc" Anderson

Longmont, Colorado

A s THE MOTORCADE escorting the body of Christopher "Doc" Anderson made its way toward his hometown, about an hour away from the Denver airport, the three sailors who served as pallbearers jumped into a white van, which then pulled in behind the limousines.

Police officers and firemen saluted as they left the airport, bathed in the flashing emergency lights.

"This is so cool that they do this," said Storekeeper Third Class Ben Engelman. "This is so amazing."

At one freeway exit, fire trucks and ambulances parked on the overpass, lights flashing. As the procession exited the interstate, the lights burned even brighter.

Along the highway, cars pulled over, along with firefighters who continued to salute.

Then there was Longmont's Main Street.

At Twentieth Avenue and Main, the flags began: kids holding plastic flags, Korean War veterans holding worn American flags, bandana-clad Vietnam veterans holding POW/MIA flags.

At Eighteenth and Main, groups held candles and signs. GOD BLESS YOUR SON. THANK YOU. A boy held his candle to his mother's to light it as the hearse passed.

At Seventeenth and Main, hands over hearts. Hats over hearts.

"Dude, this is giving me chicken skin," Petty Officer Rick Lopez said, shivering inside the van. "I've never seen anything like this."

At Fifteenth and Main, people came out of a restaurant to watch the procession. The blue lights of police cars and the red lights of medical cars shone on the Christmas decorations wrapping the trees of downtown.

Outside it was about 40 degrees. Still, the crowds continued to line the streets: more children with wobbly salutes, a woman with a walker, a couple who embraced in a hug as soon as the hearse passed.

They drove in silence for a few minutes, and then Petty Officer Lopez spoke again. "You know," he said, "sometimes I wish they would do this for us when we come home alive."

INSIDE THE FUNERAL HOME, a few feet from her son's casket, Debra Anderson held tight to a single photo.

"I had to have my picture of my smiling Christopher," she said, staring at the photo and then at the casket.

While Christopher was deployed, his parents talked with him at least once a week—mostly for only a few minutes.

"You could hear his smile in his voice. You could hear it on the phone," his father said. "He was going back to work, back to do his job, back to doing what he wanted to do."

Inside the funeral home, Debra leaned into her husband of twenty-six years, wiping her face with a tissue.

"My boy, my boy," she said. "Christopher said he'd be okay. He promised he'd be safe, Rick—he *promised* me. I miss him. I miss the phone calls. I miss him terribly. I want to talk to him."

"Hey," Rick said softly, "now we can talk to him anytime we want."

"Ooooh," she moaned. "My heart hurts. My heart *hurts*. It was my job to take care of him. I shouldn't have let him go. I shouldn't have let him go."

"You were going to stop Christopher?" his father asked. "Since when?"

They both managed a smile, and their eyes again fell on the casket.

As the family told Christopher stories from chairs in a corner of the room, the corpsman's younger brother, Kyle, stood at the foot of the casket, refusing to leave his place, patting the rough, wrinkled flag.

The brothers had grown up as opposites: Christopher the well-dressed go-getter and Kyle the rebel who shopped at thrift stores.

They fought like most brothers fight. Sometimes, they fought worse than most brothers fight. They hadn't spoken while he was in Iraq.

As the family continued to share stories, sniffling and laughing, Kyle refused to move from the casket.

"Why don't you come over here with us?" Rick asked him. "Why are you standing there all alone?"

Kyle looked at his father, his eyes red, and patted the casket again. "I'm not alone," he said.

More than sixteen hours after John Dragneff's day began, the skinny sailor walked into the room and handed Christopher's parents a condolence card:

Instead of saying, "I'm sorry for your loss," I wanted to say, "Thank you" for Christopher. We claimed each other as brothers.

"You did good, John," Rick said. "You did good."

Debra Anderson grasped the young man's hand and looked into his eyes.

"I'm glad you came with him. It's what he wanted. You did a good job. You got him home," she said, gripping his hand even tighter. "Thank you for bringing him home."

21

Marine Corporal
Brett Lee Lundstrom

Pine Ridge Indian Reservation, South Dakota

W HICH ONE IS it?"

Doyla Lundstrom screamed into the telephone, not knowing which of her deployed sons was dead.

Finally, her former husband managed a single word: "Brett."

Two weeks later, two miles from the Pine Ridge Indian Reservation, two Marines in a rental car tuned their FM radio to the reservation's station, which crackled and then locked onto the signal.

"I understand they are currently escorting Brett's body back," the disc jockey said. "There are several police cars, followed by the hearse and vans filled with Marines. We'll let you know when they are on the reservation."

The two Marines from Colorado stared out at the road that

wound through the rolling brown grass of the desolate Badlands. A few cars ahead, through the back window of the hearse, they could see the flag-draped casket of the first Oglala Sioux fatality of the war in Iraq.

The disc jockey broke in again a few minutes later: "Right now they are at the reservation line with the body of Corporal Brett Lundstrom," she said. "I've got eight songs queued up here, and we will play them back to back. So here they are, going out to Corporal Lundstrom . . ."

She started with a spoken word piece that began just as the procession rolled across the reservation line.

"Throughout time, American Indians have had to defend themselves and their way of life," said the solemn voice of songwriter Wil Numkena. *"American Indian warriors have a long tradition of protecting their families, tribe, and nation . . ."*

The Marines listened as they drove past weather-beaten wooden houses and lone mobile homes, through one of the poorest counties in the United States, toward the geographic center of the two-million-acre reservation.

"By tradition, American Indian people have always embraced their warriors upon their return from battle. Embraced them in heart, embraced them in spirit . . ."

Since arriving at Doyla Lundstrom's home in nearby Black Hawk to inform her of Brett's death, Marines had spent two days helping with plans for a nonstop forty-two-hour wake on the reservation—the beginning of nearly five full days of traditional honors.

Residents poured from their homes as the procession advanced. The hearse passed families sitting on the hoods of their cars, their children wrapped in colorful blankets. One couple stood at the side of the road, their heads bowed. A boy on horseback watched with his dog near a barbed-wire fence. A man in a rusty pickup stared from atop a grassy hill.

The procession continued to grow as cars from the side of the road pulled in, stretching the line for more than five miles.

On their car radios the tribute continued: *"We mourn but honor the warriors who have given of their lives in the field of battle. We embrace their spirit, for they are our very breath of life. Great Spirit, we ask of you to receive our warriors."*

BESIDE THE ROAD, three tribal chiefs in feathered headdresses waited on horseback, along with a dozen other riders and a small empty wooden wagon.

The procession arrived from over a hill, and as the Marines got out, the two bands of warriors nodded to each other. The Marines lifted the flag-draped casket from the new Cadillac hearse, transferred it to the old pinewood wagon, and fell in line, issuing clipped commands under their breath. They stood at attention in spotless dress blue uniforms, white gloves, and shiny black dress shoes. The Oglala Sioux escorts wore blue jeans, windbreakers, and dusty boots. They spoke to their horses in the Lakota language.

"Unkiyapo," someone said. "Let's go."

They walked together, the Marines marching in crisp formation behind the chiefs. A splotchy old paint horse ambled along behind them all. In a funeral tradition that goes back generations, its saddle was empty.

The procession was quiet, other than occasional war whoops and horse whinnies, until it reached the gym at Little Wound High School at the center of the tiny town of Kyle. In the parking lot of the school one woman sat alone in her car, crying.

Then the drumbeat began.

Inside the gymnasium, "Home of the Mustangs," a thirty-foot-tall tepee stretched above one end of the hardwood floor, reaching nearly to the free-throw line.

The Marines brought the flag-draped casket to the front of the tepee. Two of them took their post at each end, beginning a shift that would last for the next two days.

Several rows of elderly men slowly moved forward, some supported by gnarled canes. Others had pulled their hair into dark gray ponytails, framing faces that looked like the landscape. Many wore old caps and uniforms stitched with distinctive patches—Airborne, Special Forces, and the revered combat infantry badge—along with dozens of gleaming medals. On the back of their caps, some also wore a single eagle feather.

At the front of the tepee, a funeral director opened the casket.

CORPORAL BRETT LEE Lundstrom grew up in the wake of warriors. Among his distant relations was Dewey Beard, also known by the Lakota Sioux name Iron Hail, who fought in the Battle of the Little Bighorn and survived the 1890 massacre at Wounded Knee, not far from where Brett was born. A grandfather on his father's side was Red Cloud, one of the great Lakota leaders of the 1800s.

More recently, his great-uncle, Charlie Under Baggage, was killed at the Battle of the Bulge during World War II. Another great-uncle, Alfred Under Baggage, was killed in Korea. He had relatives at the Pine Ridge Indian Reservation who served in Vietnam and Desert Storm. Then there was his father, who retired as a Marine major.

In January 2003 he asked for the most dangerous job in the Marine Corps, one that would almost certainly send him into battle.

"I always told him he volunteered twice. Not only did he volunteer as a Marine, he volunteered to be infantry," Ed Lundstrom Sr. said. "I tried to talk him out of it. He had so many other options besides enlisting. But he knew what he was getting into. He went into it with eyes wide open."

Next to the casket in the Pine Ridge gym, a tribe member placed a tall staff crested with buffalo hair and lined with eagle feathers to represent local members of the tribe stationed in Iraq. The middle of the staff was pinned with photos of their faces: Sophia Young Bear, Jason Brave Heart, Kimberly Long Soldier, Lisa White Face . . .

Atop them all was the photo of Brett Lundstrom.

Upon their return from Iraq, tribe members receive the highest honor for bravery: an eagle feather. If they are injured in combat, the feather may be stained red with blood.

Before the first night's ceremony began, a sixty-five-year-old Vietnam veteran named John Around Him looked at the staff and then at Brett Lundstrom's flag-draped casket.

"He earns the American flag from his government," he said. "He earns the eagle feather from his people."

Near 11:00 P.M. on the first night of the wake, the gymnasium fell silent. Along with his first and last eagle feather, Brett was about to receive something even more enduring.

"This evening I want to take a few minutes of your time to name my grandson," said Birgil Kills Straight, Brett's great-uncle. "Before he enters the spirit world, it's important for him to have an Indian name, because that's how the ancestors will know him."

The tribal elder had gone to a sweat lodge earlier that night to pray for the name and to ask the spirits to guide the fallen warrior.

Long after midnight the Marines rolled Brett's body into the tepee, where Lakota beliefs hold that the spirits of Brett's ancestors would communicate with his.

First, the wise man said, they needed to know who he was.

"His name is *Wanbli Isnala*," Birgil Kills Straight said and then translated: *"Lone Eagle."*

With that he took the eagle feather, walked to the open casket, and placed it on the Marine's chest.

"He alone, above everything else, is an eagle," Birgil Kills Straight said. "He will fly to the highest reaches of the universe. He may bring back news to us in our dreams."

He looked to the stands of the gymnasium and spoke of Brett's well-known warrior ancestors.

"The blood of these people you've probably heard of runs in the blood of Brett. . . . This is who Brett is," Birgil Kills Straight said. "He is a warrior."

After placing ceremonial grasses in the casket and offering prayers in Lakota, he turned again to the crowd.

"Now I want to name my other grandson," he said.

From the back of the room Private First Class Eddy Lundstrom walked in, wearing the same desert camouflage uniform he wore only a week earlier in Tikrit when he was told of his brother's death. As the only surviving son in the family, he had the option of spending the rest of his tour stateside. Instead, he would return to Iraq in less than a week.

In the days leading up to the naming ceremony, as Birgil Kills Straight searched for the proper names to bestow on the two brothers, he said he wanted a name that might help ensure Eddy's safe return.

As the twenty-one-year-old private stood at attention, his shoulders straight, his fingers curled slightly at his sides, his uncle took out another eagle feather.

"His name is *Wicahci Kailehya*," he said finally. *"Shining Star."*

MARINE LANCE CORPORAL
KYLE W. BURNS

Kyle was always proud to call himself a country boy, wearing Carhartts instead of Levi's, chewing Copenhagen so frequently that it looked like he had a pinch in his mouth even when he didn't. His frame was small but tough—perfect for his favorite sport, ice hockey. And for the Marines. He kept his friends entertained with a simple sense of humor. This was his favorite joke: "Why was six afraid of seven? Because seven ate nine." When he went out drinking, he wore a cap with rabbit-fur earflaps.

Even after Kyle's second deployment, his mother still questioned his decision to join the Corps. "I have to be honest," she said. "I didn't believe all that brotherhood bullshit. I thought it was just a bunch of little boys saying things that boys say. I never believed it until after he died."

(© ROCKY MOUNTAIN NEWS / BURNS FAMILY)

MARINE STAFF SERGEANT
THEODORE SAMUEL HOLDER II

As an accident-prone kid who was often bested in wrestling matches by his big sister, "Sammy" Holder never seemed to master his lanky legs and arms. He struggled constantly with grades, and he barely graduated from high school. In the Marine Corps, his family says, he finally grew up, emotionally and physically.

After boot camp, he drew guard duty at various U.S. embassies, where the world literally opened to him as he served in Trinidad and Tobago, Cyprus, and the Czech Republic, where he met his fiancée and planned to keep exploring.

By the time he deployed to Iraq, Sam Holder's body was as chiseled and muscular as a comic-book superhero. For his actions in the battle where he died on Veterans Day, the twenty-seven year-old was posthumously awarded the Silver Star.

"A medal cannot replace his life," said one of the men who served with him. "It's not replacing him. It represents the five or six Marines who came back because of him."

(© ROCKY MOUNTAIN NEWS / HOLDER FAMILY)

NAVY HOSPITAL CORPSMAN HM3 CHRISTOPHER "DOC" ANDERSON

The kid they would eventually call "Doc" grew up a prankster with a Bart Simpsonesque streak, a master of mooning his cousins from the car and driving schoolteachers to the brink of breakdown. But when he became the fourth generation of his family to serve in the military, he committed himself entirely.

As a Navy Corpsman, he volunteered to serve on the front lines, where he knew he was a target, since he was the only one who could save the lives of his Marines. Soon after deploying, he found himself crouched in the back of a racing Humvee, his hands covered with his sergeant's blood; his hazel eyes were the last thing the sergeant would see before passing out.

(© ROCKY MOUNTAIN NEWS / ANDERSON FAMILY)

MARINE CORPORAL BRETT L. LUNDSTROM

Brett Lundstrom grew up in the wake of warriors.

Among his distant relations was Dewey Beard, also known by the Lakota Sioux name Iron Hail, who fought in the Battle of the Little Bighorn and survived the 1890 massacre at Wounded Knee, not far from where Brett was born. A grandfather on his father's side was Red Cloud, one of the great Lakota leaders of the 1800s.

In January 2003 he asked for the most dangerous job in the Marine Corps—one that would almost certainly send him into battle.

"I always told him he volunteered twice. Not only did he volunteer as a Marine, he volunteered to be infantry," Ed Lundstrom Sr. said. "I tried to talk him out of it. He had so many other options besides enlisting. But he knew what he was getting into. He went into it eyes wide open."

(© ROCKY MOUNTAIN NEWS / LUNDSTROM FAMILY)

MARINE SECOND LIEUTENANT JAMES J. CATHEY

Jim Cathey was a champion kickboxer and bird hunter, but could knit and cross-stitch, and was a master at the sewing machine. As a boy, he stitched a needlepoint for his mother that read simply HOME.

When he said good-bye to his pregnant wife on the day he deployed for Iraq, he left his final promise in a letter.

"I will be home," he wrote. *"I have a wife and a new baby to take care of, and you guys are my world."*

ARMY PRIVATE FIRST CLASS JESSE A. GIVENS

Jesse Givens looked as tough as his hard hat when he headed to work, strengthened by lifting the steel that held together dams and buildings from the foundation up.

When he got home, the iron-worker was likely to pick up a charcoal pencil and sketch, finding solace in his artwork, especially art of the human form. The twisted steel of September 11, 2001, inspired him to join the Army. His wife, Melissa, was seven months pregnant when he left for Iraq. She gave birth to his son, Carson, a month after his funeral.

At their home, she picked up one of his last sketches.

"It's a picture of a little boy and a soldier," Melissa said. "He didn't finish it."

It's nearly two A.M. when Major Steve Beck hugs his wife, Julie, before leaving to conduct a casualty notification. In 2007 the Marines restricted nighttime notifications—a policy that concerns Beck. "Wouldn't you want to know as soon as you possibly could?" he asked. "If it was your son, would you want us to let you sleep?"

(© ROCKY MOUNTAIN NEWS / TODD HEISLER)

Major Steve Beck and another Marine approach Jim Cathey's family home in Reno, Nevada, preparing to escort his loved ones to the airport to receive his body. On the day Jim Cathey died, another group of Marines followed the same path, carrying the news of the twenty-four-year-old's death, now signified by a gold star in the window. On that day the Marines were met on the driveway by Jim Cathey's mother, Caroline. As soon as she saw the van, she knew. "Please don't let it be," she said. "Please tell me it's not Jimmy, please tell me it's not my son." (© ROCKY MOUNTAIN NEWS / TODD HEISLER)

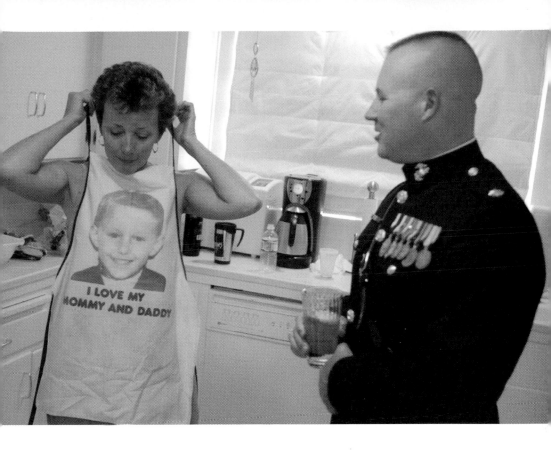

At the family home in Reno, Caroline Cathey dons an apron her son gave her when he was a child, and Jim Cathey's sister Joyce shows off a tattoo she had inked on her neck, "so he's always watching my back."

(© ROCKY MOUNTAIN NEWS / TODD HEISLER)

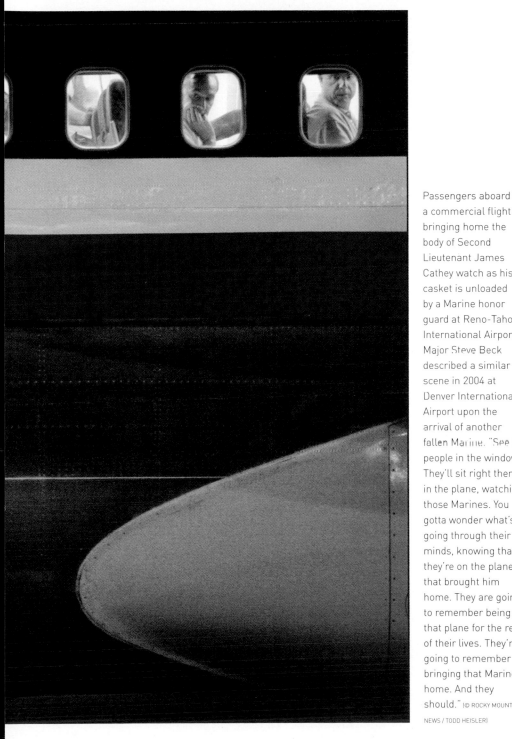

Passengers aboard a commercial flight bringing home the body of Second Lieutenant James Cathey watch as his casket is unloaded by a Marine honor guard at Reno-Tahoe International Airport. Major Steve Beck described a similar scene in 2004 at Denver International Airport upon the arrival of another fallen Marine. "See the people in the windows? They'll sit right there in the plane, watching those Marines. You gotta wonder what's going through their minds, knowing that they're on the plane that brought him home. They are going to remember being on that plane for the rest of their lives. They're going to remember bringing that Marine home. And they should." (© ROCKY MOUNTAIN NEWS / TODD HEISLER)

Major Steve Beck supports Katherine Cathey as she breaks down at the sight of her husband's casket at the airport. When Major Beck knocked on her door in Colorado to notify her of her husband's death, she had cursed him, then refused to speak to him for more than an hour. Eventually, she came to lean on him.

Major Steve Beck folds back the flag on Jim Cathey's casket during what he calls "the final inspection," where he is alone with the casket, ensuring every detail is looked after before the family enters.

Katherine presses her pregnant belly against Jim Cathey's flag-draped casket, then drapes herself over it as Major Steve Beck stands by. "I would suck all her pain away if I could. Every Marine would," he said. "They'd take every ounce of pain and just absorb it." Two days after she was notified of her husband's death, she found out the baby would be a boy. She already decided on the name: James J. Cathey Jr. [© ROCKY MOUNTAIN NEWS / TODD HEISLER]

The night before her husband's burial, Katherine Cathey refused to leave his casket, asking to sleep next to him one last time. The Marines gathered sheets, pillows, and an air mattress, setting up a makeshift bed. Before she fell asleep, Katherine opened her laptop computer and played the songs they would have listened to at the formal wedding they never held. One of the Marines asked her if she wanted them to continue standing watch as she slept. "I think it would be kind of nice if you kept doing it," she said. "I think that's what he would have wanted." [© ROCKY MOUNTAIN NEWS / TODD HEISLER]

While stationed in Hawaii, Jim Cathey and his Marine buddies took a trip to Iwo Jima, where they camped on the same beach the Marines stormed during World War II, sacrificing nearly six thousand of their lives. After camping on that beach, the young Marines each took a bagful of sand from Iwo Jima. At the end of Jim Cathey's funeral, his buddies removed the formal white dress gloves they used to carry him for the last time. They then took fistfuls of sand and drizzled it over his casket. The sand, they said, represented all who had been lost more than six decades earlier. "Now," said one of the Marines, "they can be part of him, too."

[© ROCKY MOUNTAIN NEWS / TODD HEISLER]

Andrew Alonzo touches up the paint on the gravestone of Marine Lance Corporal Kyle Burns, who was killed on Veterans Day of 2004. Alonzo, a former Marine and sergeant in the Army Reserves, had only recently returned from a tour of duty in Iraq, where one of his best friends died. Despite constant reminders of the war—reminders that even drove him to contemplate suicide —he says he finds solace in his job as a caretaker at Fort Logan National Cemetery, where he sets the stones for all the troops who did not make it home alive. (© ROCKY MOUNTAIN NEWS /CHRIS SCHNEIDER)

Jo Burns weeps as her husband, Bob, unpacks a box containing their son's uniforms that Major Steve Beck, right, brought from Denver. "For me, having all this back is a good thing," Jo Burns said. "I don't ever want to forget or to stop feeling." "I don't want to forget, either," Bob Burns said. "I just don't want to hurt."

(© ROCKY MOUNTAIN NEWS / TODD HEISLER)

During a ceremony to award posthumous medals to the families of the fallen, called Remembering the Brave, Jo Burns, right, held tight to Corporal Dustin Barker, one of the last men to see her son alive.

During a Remembering the Brave ceremony, Major Steve Beck holds a medal that will never be worn. Often, posthumous medals arrive in loose envelopes in the mail. Beck, along with a mother who lost her son in Iraq, created an organization that presents the medals in a formal ceremony he says that every family deserves. "It's not an ending. It's not a period at the end of their lives," Major Beck said of the medals. "It's a semicolon. The story will continue to be told."

Two bands of warriors met on the Pine Ridge Indian Reservation in 2005 to welcome home the body of Marine Lance Corporal Brett Lundstrom, the first Oglala Lakota Sioux tribe member killed in Iraq. The Marines transferred the flag-draped casket to a horse-drawn clapboard wagon, which was followed by hundreds of residents of the reservation. The procession began a nonstop wake that would last nearly two days, accompanied by a constant, steady drumbeat. [© ROCKY MOUNTAIN NEWS / TODD HEISLER]

The shadows cast by Lakota warriors stretch for centuries. Native Americans have the highest per-capita percentage of participation in the military—a statistic many credit to the history of protecting the tribe. Many of the elaborate headdresses, or war bonnets, are passed down through generations. (© ROCKY MOUNTAIN NEWS / TODD HEISLER)

Inside the gymnasium of Little Wound High School on the Pine Ridge Indian Reservation,
Brett Lundstrom's body was placed inside an enormous teepee. Once inside the teepee,
it is believed that his spirit can communicate with the spirits of his ancestors.

Captain Chris Sutherland hands Doyla and Ed Lundstrom the watch that their son wore when the Marine was killed. In Sutherland's left hand, he holds a red velvet bag he will give to Lundstrom's mother. Inside the bag are her son's dog tags. (© ROCKY MOUNTAIN NEWS /MARC PISCOTTY)

One week after his brother's funeral, Army Specialist Eddy Lundstrom headed back to Iraq. After returning home several months later, he refused to visit his brother's grave as he struggled with his own emotions. Finally, he decided to come to Fort Logan National Cemetery in Denver. "I want to have a beer with my brother," he said.

(© ROCKY MOUNTAIN NEWS / TODD HEISLER)

Melissa and Dakota Givens watch a message videotaped by Jesse Givens the night before he left for Iraq. "I'm with you all the time. My heart's with you, my mind's with you. My soul's with you," he said. "You're my family. You've made me happier than I could ever be, and I'll be home as soon as I can." [© ROCKY MOUNTAIN NEWS / EVAN SEMON]

Carson Givens sleeps under a portrait of the father he never met. Some nights, the toddler says he sees his daddy in his dreams.

To help heal her son's grief, Melissa Givens inflated helium balloons and wrote messages on them. "We're going to send the balloons to heaven," Melissa said."So my dad can read them there," the boy said.

Jesse Givens's last letter home was found in the tank where he drowned, his last words ripped apart. He had written and mailed other copies of the "just in case" letter so that his wife, son Dakota, and the child that was born after he died would know his feelings: *"Bean, I never got to see you but I know in my heart you are beautiful. I will always have with me the feel of the soft nudges on your mom's belly, and the joy I felt when we found out you were on the way. I dream of you every night, and I always will. Don't ever think that since I wasn't around that I didn't love you. You were conceived of love and I came to this terrible place for love. Please understand that I had to be gone so that I could take care of my family. I love you Bean."*

Kyle Anderson kisses his brother's casket at Arlington National Cemetery. At every opportunity to hold his brother's casket, Kyle Anderson stayed the longest. At one point, his father asked, "Why don't you come over here with us? Why are you standing there all alone?" Kyle replied simply, "I'm not alone." [© ROCKY MOUNTAIN NEWS / CHRIS SCHNEIDER]

After saluting the casket of his best friend, Navy Hospital Corpsman John Dragneff could no longer hold back the tears as he stood on the chilly tarmac in Philadelphia. Before Christopher Anderson left for Iraq, he requested that if he died, John would be the one to escort his body home to Colorado. "Even though we were best friends, this isn't for me," John said. "This is for the family." (© ROCKY MOUNTAIN NEWS / CHRIS SCHNEIDER)

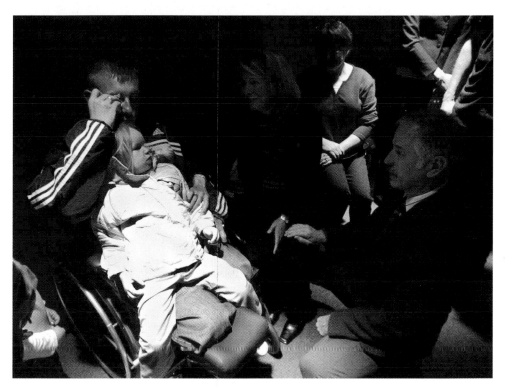

Marine Sergeant Gregory Edwards wipes a tear as he meets the parents of the man he says saved his life. Though he lost both legs in the explosion and was still in recovery, he wanted to attend the funeral at Arlington National Cemetery. "Your boy kept me alive," the sergeant told Rick and Debra Anderson. "If it wasn't for him, I wouldn't be here. I wouldn't be able to hold my daughter on my lap."

James J."Jimmy" Cathey Jr. was born December 22, 2005: 7 pounds, 10 ounces. After spending his first two days in the nursery, Jimmy was allowed to spend Christmas Eve in his mother's room, their first night together. "He has the nose. One of his ears sticks out more than the other like his dad. He has these really long fingers and feet like Jim," Katherine said. "And he smiles. He smiles a lot." (© ROCKY MOUNTAIN NEWS TODD HEISLER)

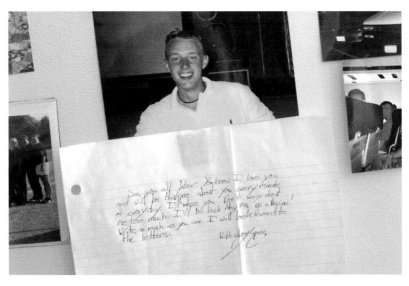

Inside Jim Cathey's family home in Reno, Nevada, the same note has hung on the refrigerator since the day he left for boot camp: "*See you all later. You know I love you and will be thinking about you every minute of every day. I miss you. Don't worry about me too much. I'll be back May 8th as a Marine! Write as much as you can. I will look forward to the letters. With all my love, J.C.*" (© ROCKY MOUNTAIN NEWS / JUDY DEHAAS)

. . .

AMERICAN INDIANS HAVE the highest per capita participation in the armed services of any ethnic group.

"People always ask, why do the Indian people, who were treated so badly, step forward to serve their country?" James Shaw Sr. said during one of the ceremonies. "It's that good old nation pride."

For John Around Him, an Army combat infantry veteran whose son recently returned from Iraq, the bond is more tangible.

"In 1876, the Lakota Sioux took that flag from Custer," he said, nodding toward the U.S. flag near the casket. "So that flag is ours, too."

Still, after so many centuries of battle, they also know the consequences all too well.

"I saw his name on CNN, and I let out a war whoop," said Velma Killsback—whose daughter served in Iraq—as she looked at the casket that held Corporal Lundstrom. "I sat here in disbelief, wondering why. For a war that shouldn't go on."

On the reservation the war in Iraq is largely unpopular, but the men and women fighting it never are.

"When we [had] late-night talks, he would tell me how he was fighting for me to do the things I do in everyday life," said Brett's cousin Amanda Munoz. "No matter how much I was against it, I gradually understood. No matter how much I hated it and said, 'Please, Brett, don't go,' he was doing what he wanted to do. It was his calling."

. . .

IN THE WAKE'S thirtieth hour, eyes sagged, clothes had rumpled, and stubble covered the faces of many male mourners, but the energy level never waned.

Periodically, drum groups formed circles that pulled the drowsy from the bleachers. Visitors ate buffalo soup and fry bread. While most tribe members left each night to return home, some slept on the gym floor or under the bleachers, refusing to leave the man few of them had ever met.

All the while, the group of twelve young Marines from Colorado—most of whom had never visited an Indian reservation—continued to post watch in thirty-minute shifts. They stood without flinching, listening to relatives cry over the open casket, watching as friends and family members placed letters, a rose, and a hockey jersey alongside his body.

One night, while many of their friends back in Colorado watched the Denver Broncos playoff game, the Marines watched childhood photos of Brett Lundstrom's life projected on a screen next to his open casket. After the ceremony on the reservation, they would head back to Colorado for his burial at Fort Logan National Cemetery.

"I hope they will take this message back, that they'll say, 'We went to Pine Ridge, and it was one of the greatest honors we've ever seen,'" John Around Him said. "They're witnesses, to take this honor and share it."

According to Staff Sergeant Kevin Thomas, they had no choice but to carry that message. "I was a history major. I learned about the western expansion, I learned about the Indians," he said, "but I never really understood."

As the ceremony progressed, many of the mourners brought handmade gifts, including elaborate dreamcatchers, miniature illuminated tepees, and traditional star quilts. By Sunday night more than fifty of the quilts—which can take weeks to make and can sell for between $300 and $600 each—lined an entire wall of the gymnasium.

Then, as is customary, the family gave them all away.

"Value doesn't mean nothing to the family. Earthly property, it doesn't mean nothing right now. It's life that has worth," said eighty-two-year-old Sylvester Bad Cob, a World War II and Korean War veteran. "They give it out now, but they'll get it back someday."

One by one the family called up everyone who had helped organize the ceremony and presented each one with a star quilt. They began with the Marines.

"I had a picture of this in my mind, but to actually see it . . . It's just overwhelming," said Captain Chris Sutherland shortly after Doyla and Ed Lundstrom wrapped him in one of the quilts, and—as they did with each of the Marines—sealed their gift with a hug.

"If you think about it, in our culture we give thank-you notes," Captain Sutherland said, shaking his head. "Just thank-you notes."

The captain then realized he also had something to return. As the gym once again quieted, the Marine took out a small red velvet bag and walked toward Brett's parents.

He dropped to one knee and tilted the bag. He then pulled out a watch—the same one that the corporal was wearing when he was killed. He handed it to Ed Lundstrom, who had remained awake, watching his son's casket, for the past thirty-six hours. The former Marine major held tight to the watch and then crumbled in tears.

Sutherland tipped the bag again and folded the remaining contents into the hands of Brett Lundstrom's mother: her son's dog tags.

N EAR MIDNIGHT, A sixty-five-year-old Navy veteran named Regina Brave stood up in the bleachers and made her way to the floor.

"As a rule, I don't go to wakes, I don't go to funerals. But for some reason I had to come to this one," she said. "After I heard about him, I knew I had to be here. I walked for a long time."

Two days earlier she had hitchhiked more than one hundred miles across the reservation to attend the wake. She carried one of her handmade star quilts in memory of her son, a Marine who had served in the first Gulf War. It was one of the many quilts the family gave away that night.

"My father told me, 'Everywhere you go, you're there for a reason,'" she said. "'You're either there to help somebody, or they're there to help you.'"

Now she joined more than a hundred men and women who

lined up behind the Colorado Marines for the last official ceremony of the wake, the Final Roll Call.

The formation included men and women aged nineteen to
ninety. Some hobbled with walkers; others stood in desert camouflage; some wore the same clothes they had for the past two days.
As Sunday stretched into Monday, they came to attention.

For the next fifteen minutes they all waited for their name and
then barked the same response:

"Adolph Bull Bear."

"Here, sir."

"Guy Dull Knife."

"Here, sir."

"Regina Brave."

"Here, sir," each of them said one after another until they
reached the last veteran in the building.

"Corporal Brett Lee Lundstrom . . .

"Corporal Brett Lee Lundstrom . . .

"Corporal Brett Lee Lundstrom."

Finally, Captain Sutherland answered: "Not here, sir," he said.

As the Lakota warrior songs began, John Around Him took the
microphone once more.

"This ceremony will continue on because in the past, in our
history with our great warriors and how they defended our land,
their culture, and their way of life, it passes on, generation after
generation," he said. "These veterans, they love us. They care
for us."

He looked over at the groups of old men and women, and the groups of young ones, and thought of all the wars in between.

"To all the veterans who are here tonight, welcome home," he said.

Then he looked over at the open casket at the man with a feather on his chest and said it again.

"Welcome home."

22

Caroline and Jeff Cathey

Reno, Nevada

IN THE HOUSE where Jim Cathey grew up, a tattered stuffed animal peered from a heavy wooden chest.

"This is Floppy Floyd," his mother said. "The last time he was here, he said he wanted to take Floyd back, for the baby."

She held the stuffed animal to her face. Elsewhere in the house she had all of Jim's baby teeth and every award he had ever won.

On his bookshelf, encyclopedias were shelved near the Louis L'Amour novels she used to read to him, next to a collection of Thucydides' writings.

"These are the things that made him who he is today," she said and then caught herself in present tense.

"Who he *was* today," she corrected herself softly.

Caroline Cathey was one of the few mothers who never feared a call at 1:30 in the morning.

"When I heard the ring, I knew he was DD: drunk dialing," she said. "I'd wake up, pick up the phone, and he'd say, 'Hi, Mom, just wanted to say hi. We're out having a drink, and we thought we'd have a drink on you.'"

Then inevitably she would get the serenade:

"He would get all the guys together in the bar, or wherever, and have all of them singing 'Sweet Caroline' to me over the phone."

She looked over the clothes in his closet that he had left behind, including his old high school Marines jacket and a collection of shirts. She stopped at his favorite Halloween costume, which he wore even before it was finished.

"When I made this for him, he would run off the bus each day asking if it was ready," she said, holding it up. The Cowardly Lion.

She walked over to a needlepoint he had made for her—a simple house stitched with the word HOME.

"He was always better at needlepoint than I was," she said. "He always had more patience. Still, I could help him even when he got older. Here's this great big kid going, 'Mom, I don't know how to pick up this stitch.'"

Later, in the kitchen, she paused at a note that has hung on the refrigerator since the day he left home.

See you all later. You know I love you and will be thinking about you every minute of every day. I miss you. Don't worry about me too much. I'll be back May 8th as a Marine! Write as much as you can. I will look forward to the letters. With all my love,

J.C.

Jeff Cathey almost didn't make it to his son's funeral. From the moment he saw the Marines at the door, he was thinking that the next funeral might be his own.

Jeff suffers from clinical depression, which spiraled deeper the day the Marines came to the house. During those first few days, his family worried more about him than their own grief. His wife hid all his guns. Even so, the day after he found out about his son's death, he insisted on going back to the hunting grounds where he and Jim had spent their best times together.

"Before he left, I made him swear on his son's life that he would come back to me," Caroline said.

"I thought about doing it, ending it," Jeff said, breaking into tears. "I really did. I want to be with him."

As he sat on the couch, he tried to compose himself.

"Good thoughts," he told himself. "Good thoughts." And then he found plenty.

"One of my finest memories was when we were hunting and he came back to the car, overturned a pail, sat down, and started doing his homework. I wish I had a picture of that."

"You do," his wife said, rubbing his back and pointing to his head. "Right up here."

The night before the funeral, Jeff Cathey shook hands again with all of them. He found Major Beck in a corner and shared more of the stories. Then he placed a heavy hand on the major's shoulder.

"Today someone asked me what my son taught me. He taught me that you need to have more than one friend," he said, shaking his head.

Beck held out a hand. "You've got another one right here," he said.

23

Katherine Cathey

Reno, Nevada

I
N THE MORTUARY the night before Jim Cathey's funeral, two Marines stood near the casket, unfurling sheets on a makeshift bed.

"Make it look nice, dude. Make it look nice," one of them said.

"Who are you, Martha Stewart?" the other shot back with a grin.

Another looked at the blanket.

"If you're pregnant, do you get hot or cold?"

One of the Marines who has a child of his own looked at the bed.

"She's going to need another pillow," he said. "Since she's pregnant, she'll need to put a pillow between her legs."

Then they saw car lights outside and took their positions.

Earlier that day, Katherine had told them she couldn't bear to spend the last night away from her husband. She said she would sleep on a pew if she had to. The Marines found her an air mattress instead and promised to be ready.

Arriving exhausted, she almost immediately crawled onto the bed they had made for her. Her stepfather helped tuck her in.

"Do you have another pillow?" she asked. "I need one to put between my legs."

One of the Marines crouched down and asked if they should continue to post guard in the room.

"We can do whatever you want," he said. "We can stay or we can give you some privacy."

"I think it would be kind of nice if you kept doing it," she said. "I think that's what he would have wanted."

A Marine dimmed the lights, and Katherine opened a laptop computer on the floor. In the blue glow of the screen, she listened to the songs they would have played at the wedding they never had, songs that spanned Rascal Flatts to Billy Joel.

She swayed and then closed her eyes.

As drowsiness set in, she picked up an old T-shirt, the last shirt Jim Cathey wore before changing into his cammies to leave for Iraq. She hadn't washed it. It still smelled like him.

She held the shirt to her face and breathed in.

24

Jim Cathey's Marines

Reno, Nevada

As Katherine slept, Staff Sergeant Andrew Price walked to the back of the room and dimmed the lights even further. For the next hour he stood guard until another Marine approached from the shadows. The new Marine stood in front of the makeshift bed, gave a slow salute, and then walked to Price, relieving him. After every watch, each Marine shed his dress blues for a white T-shirt and walked to a small dark room in the back of the funeral home. Lit only by the glow of a newspaper reporter's computer screen, they began to speak:

1:37 A.M.: Staff Sergeant Andrew Price
We would have stayed as long as Katherine wanted us there tonight. Even if she wanted us to go, I would have stayed there for

her. I would have walked around in the shadows. Some way or another we're always going to try to take care of her. Wherever she needs to go, all she needs to say is that [her] husband died in Iraq. They'll take her under their wing. And her child. It's something that this country hasn't had to deal with. But there's going to be a whole generation that doesn't know their father. . . .

It's almost selfish of us to die. They train us as warriors. They don't teach us how to take the pain away. . . .

I'm glad that I had this opportunity to do this for Cat but also for myself. In the Marine Corps we always talk about "Never leave a brother behind." You hear that; you hear about the flag-draped casket. We just want to know that we're never going to be left. It's just a little peace of mind—that it doesn't just end violently and that's the end of it.

2:28 A.M.: Second Lieutenant Charlie Loya

Kat called on Monday, and I was on predeployment leave. She called pretty much hysterical. She said, "Cat's dead, Cat's dead." I said, "Who is this?" And she said, "It's Kat. Cat's dead." I said, "Where's he at?" I said, "How do you know he's dead?" She said two Marines in dress blues came by.

I'm the joker of the group, I love busting balls, and I talk a lot of shit. Now I'm leaving messages that say, "I've got a huge emergency, dude. I'm not joking around." They said, "Quit fucking around, Charlie." They'd say, "How do you know?"

I said, "Kat got the dress blues visit . . ."

People would ask me how I'm doing, and I'd say I'm fine. And

I was. Then when they put him on that conveyor belt [at the airport], man, it was tough. I got the chills. I felt like, honored. Holy shit, the airline's not letting the people off the plane. I was like, "This is the way it should be," and I didn't expect anything less. It was just, "This is what it's all about right now."

We picked the casket up off the conveyor belt, and all I heard was Katherine screaming, and the waterworks started. I thought, "My wife would be doing the same thing." Then all I could think about was my son. He's my everything. Now I'm fucking scared. People would ask how I felt about going over there. I'd say, "I'm confident, I'm prepared, and my boys are ready." Now I'm fucking scared.

Whenever a family member starts crying, I think of my wife and my kids. That's what I think about whenever I hear a woman crying. I think about my wife, Nicole. Before I went to bed this morning or last night or whenever it was, I finally talked to her. Over the past couple days she's asked, and I'll say "I'm fine," [and] try to get off the subject. This morning I actually broke down. She started crying. That's not what I wanted. I just said, "I gotta go." She said, "Why?" and I just kind of made something up. She doesn't need to worry about it, you know. I pretty much ended the phone call. I try not to get my wife too worked up about it. . . .

At first [after hearing the news] I was really pissed. I didn't have any answers. At first you think, "What was he doing in the front?" Then you think, "Leadership by example," but then you think, "That wasn't his job." I was a little upset with him. . . . And then every time I pick him up [in the casket], I think of my wife and kids. The second day we went to the mass. Folding that flag, Jon and I, I thought I was going to pass out. And, again, pissed off.

When I say I'm pissed off, it's just because I don't have anything else to say.

3:19 A.M.: Staff Sergeant David Rubio

Me and Cat were really similar, just cocky, arrogant bastards. He was the smartest dumb guy I knew. I used to always tell him that. Just a big oaf. I was shocked that he was actually intelligent.

I can see myself doing the same thing he did, leading my Marines into a building. But you can't think about it too much. It's not good. When you're in college, you're so detached from what's happening in Iraq. You're worried about classes.

During your military career you will stand thousands of hours of watch, but having to salute your buddy's casket while stories go through your mind— I keep seeing that face, that big cheesy face. It was emotional standing there.

I got a call from him a couple months ago. We shot the shit. The last thing he said was "Mark time, dude. Mark time. I'll see you in the fleet."

It just basically means "I'll be waiting for you."

3:56 A.M.: Second Lieutenant John Lloyd

I've been to a few funerals, some of them family, and they're all kind of on a happy note, that they were able to live their lives to their fullest and pass away peacefully. It's tough to come out here when . . . [His voice trailed off.]

Before I came out, I was already drained emotionally. The best thing I could do all week was just keep training to keep it off my mind. Here it's the only thing you can think of. And seeing Katherine out there right now is tough. It's just a nightmare you wish you could wake up from. I'm sure Katherine is thinking the same thing. This is her last chance where she can wake up and he'll be there. . . .

I haven't really said good-bye. I guess I haven't had time. I was standing post for a good hour and then extra post after that. I have said good-bye as far as toasting three or four times. I'm not a formal good-bye sayer because—Well, I never liked good-byes anyway.

4:23 A.M.: *Second Lieutenant Jon Mueller*

Nobody knew what would happen. I didn't think it would be this—not physical, but I'm just wore out from this. It's not hard work, but it's just—it's hard. . . .

The airport was my punch to the face. The initial shock was, this is pretty heavy. Our instructions were, as soon as we saw the conveyor belt, to go up. It was just strange seeing all those people looking. All those faces. I tried to tune it out. . . .

I felt so bad for Katherine—sleeping with her husband one last time. It's so powerful. You wish you could actually do something, but all you can offer is support. You feel helpless.

It hit home, and it hit home for me, too. But I'm still going to go [to Iraq] when they ask me to go. But I also want people to know what I am doing. I'm not a very emotional guy, I don't show emotion, but I know that it's important for people to know how much you care for them. I'm not the kind of guy who can say "I love you." It's not easy for me.

It'll— I'll make it so that my loved ones know that I love them.

5:19 A.M.: Second Lieutenant Jason Lindauer

We were getting ready to go out to the field. There was a message from Charlie. I could tell from his voice that it wasn't good. He said, "Cat's gone." I said, "What?" He said, "Cat's been hit by an IED [improvised explosive device]." I said, "What?" He had to tell me like six times. I said, "Quit fucking around, Charlie."

[The first night on watch] I just spent a lot of time looking at [the casket], just trying to wrap my mind around it. To picture it. Also, the casket is my own mortality. . . .

I've known guys who made it through [officer training school] and thought, "How did they make it? These guys are going to get someone killed or get killed themselves." I never thought that about Cat. He was designed to do what he was doing. That's what he was made for. Now I'm just thinking about, well, it can happen to anybody if it can happen to Cat. And thinking about the event itself that killed him, because I was trying to picture what happened and the injuries he received. We all hoped he hadn't suffered. . . . Right now it just feels like someone's taken a vacuum and sucked everything out. . . .

At TBS [The Basic School in Quantico] they tell you you'll have to make these decisions and send the thing that you love to die, which is your Marines. You'll have to kill the ones that you love. And you'll have to share the risk, though to a lesser degree [as an officer]. . . .

Not that you couldn't get killed driving down the road, but of course this is higher risk. The reality of what we're going to be doing over there has made it more real. And to be honest, it's made it a little more scary. Watching it on the news, I never really thought about it, because I thought, "I'll deploy, and [these deaths] are unfortunate, but it's happening to other people." But for Cat to get smoked . . . They say if you spend enough time in the military, you'll know someone who died. I never thought it would be this soon. . . .

I've really been more of a family guy. My focus is, I've never put the military before my family. I automatically put myself in Jeff [Cathey]'s shoes. Because Cat and I, we were a lot alike. We both loved the outdoors. Fishing. My oldest boy is to the point where I can start to do those things. He enjoys fishing. Playing ball with him, pitching the ball to him. Just the interaction, things we've done with him so far. He's only four. Add twenty years to that, and I can't imagine the loss. I already understand the father-son dynamic, the emotion that's involved with my boy. I think if that [happened] to me, I don't think I could maintain my sanity.

Cat was doing what he loved. I suppose that makes it a little easier, but . . . I called my son on the phone, and he said, "Daddy, my friend Cat got killed." My wife had told him.

I said, "Yeah, I know, buddy. Cat's in heaven."

[The Marine started to cry.]

He said, "Well, when's he coming back?"

[He cried more, barely managing the next words.]

I said, "He's not, buddy."

A S THE SUN rose in Reno, the casinos continued to chime. Diners began to fill. In the newspapers that hit the porches, Iraq had been pushed to the back pages again.

On the busy street outside the funeral home, cars rushed by on the morning commute, their passengers oblivious to the scene inside the chapel.

While the city churned, the sun found the building where Katherine Cathey awoke.

"It's the best night of sleep I've had," she said, surprised. "I really slept."

She sat wrapped in a blanket, her eyes bleary, looking at the casket.

"You take for granted the last night you spend with them," she said. "I think I took it for granted. This was the last night I'll have to sleep next to him."

Behind her the next Marine approached, preparing to take over the watch.

"I feel like they're my angels looking over me," Katherine said.

She placed her hand on her belly.

"Looking over us," she said.

. . .

I

T STARTED IN slow motion. At a windswept cemetery near Second Lieutenant Jim Cathey's favorite hunting grounds, the Marines moved with deliberate precision, taking their time, as slow as each final salute.

Major Beck stood back and started the ritual again.

"Present military honors," he commanded.

In the distance, seven members of the rifle guard from Reno readied their weapons. Because the unit was so small—with many of its members in Iraq—they had called in recruiters and other Marines from across the state.

"Ready. Aim. Fire."

With each volley almost everyone in the shelter flinched.

"Ready. Aim. Fire."

The Marines at the casket held steady.

"Ready. Aim. Fire."

They knew the hard part was still to come.

Taps.

The Marines held the flag as the bugler played. One of the lieutenants blinked almost continuously, trying to hold back the tears. After the last note, they began to fold.

The pallbearers had spent more than an hour the day before with Major Beck as he instructed them on how to fold the flag. For such a seemingly simple task, there are hundreds of ways to get it wrong, especially when you're folding it for your friend's pregnant wife. Especially when you're folding his flag for the last time.

The Marines took their time, stretching one fold after another into a straining, tight, permanent triangle. A sergeant walked up and slipped the still-hot shells from the rifle salute into the folded flag. Major Beck took the flag, cradling it with one hand on top, one hand below, and carried it to Katherine.

He bent down on one knee, looking at his hands and at the flag, his eyes reddening. Before his tears could spill, his face snapped up, and he looked her in the eyes.

"Katherine," he said. Then he said words meant only for her— words he had composed. When he was done, he stepped back into the blank stare.

Captain Winston Tierney walked forward, carrying another flag for Caroline Cathey. The night before, the Marines had used the flag to practice, draping it over the casket—not only for themselves but also so that Jim Cathey's mother would know that it had covered her son. The captain bent down on one knee, passed the flag into Caroline's hands, and then faded into the background.

Jim Cathey's friends had one more task.

The Marines, many of whom had paid their own way to fly in the night before, walked up to the casket. One by one they removed their white gloves and placed them on the smooth wood. Then they reached into a bag of black sand.

A few years ago, while stationed with the infantry in Hawaii, Jim Cathey and his friends had taken a trip to Iwo Jima, where nearly six thousand Marines had lost their lives almost sixty years before. The young Marines slept on the beach, thinking about all that had happened there. The day before they left, they each collected a bag of sand.

The bags sat in their rooms for years. Girlfriends questioned them. Wives wondered what they would ever do with them.

One by one the young Marines poured handfuls of sand onto the gloves atop the casket and then stepped back. Sergeant Gavin Conley, who had escorted his friend's body to Reno, reached into the bag, made a fist, and drizzled the grains onto the casket.

"[The day after sleeping on the beach], we all did a hike up Mount Suribachi where our battalion commander spoke, and we rendered honors to all the fallen," Sergeant Conley said.

He looked over at the sand-covered gloves on the casket.

"Now they can be part of him, too."

25

Unprepared

CASUALTY NOTIFICATION ISN'T always conducted with the same care.

In 2005, in the underbelly of the Chicago airport, Alan Patten saw his son's casket for the first time. It was presented to him on a forklift.

"It was like he was just a piece of luggage or cargo," Mr. Patten said. "I thought, 'This is the way servicemen get treated when they come home from making the ultimate sacrifice?'"

The Patten family's experience was one of many missteps by a military that was caught off guard by the number of casualties after the war began.

Another family in Illinois thought it insensitive that when informing them of their son's death, the casualty assistance officer literally read from a script. Others have watched their casualty officers "drop off the radar" or end up in Iraq with no replacement provided. In some cases, the military has taken months to pay for a funeral or left families alone to navigate the morass of paperwork that followed a service member's death.

More than two years after Lance Corporal Andrew Patten's death, his father said he still had not received some of his son's most precious possessions, including the camera containing his last photos of life in Iraq. Mr. Patten said he was initially given incorrect information about how his son died, and he had gone more than a year before hearing from his casualty assistance officer.

"They call them brothers in the service, but if this is the way you treat your fellow Marines—It just left a bad taste," he said.

Mr. Patten had expected to bring his son back to the church where he found solace and strength—the church that regularly sent enough food and supplies for his entire platoon. That faith never wavered, his father said, as he preached to his troops to the point where they called him "The Rev."

It's that faith, and a willingness to sacrifice himself, that his father says still manages to overshadow most military mistakes.

"He practiced his belief. He was razzed, even kidded about it, but at the memorial service they came forward in tears and said he knew what he stood for," his father said. "I'm extremely proud of him, for his service for God and country, as a parent. And I know I'll join him one day."

Other cases surfaced during congressional testimony by war

widows. Jennifer McCollum of Jacksonville, Florida, complained about the lack of emotional support and direction after her husband died.

"My situation is not unique, and as a matter of fact, I am discovering that casualty assistance is increasingly failing miserably and disgracefully," she told the Committee on Veterans' Affairs in 2005. "Successful casualty assistance is not the rule; it is quite the exception. Not only is there a significant lack of continuity, but casualty assistance is a 'learn as you go' for officers that otherwise have jobs that need to be done for the unit or squadron to continue and maintain. This is certainly not the military taking care of its own."

She also said she had dealt with families who had not received reimbursement for funerals—a situation she called "a prime example of families falling through the cracks in a system that is not working."

Since the start of the war in Iraq, all branches of the military have reevaluated the notification training process, and some offer daylong courses on casualty notification. After the death of Army Ranger and former Arizona Cardinals football player Pat Tillman— whose family was initially informed that he died heroically in a battle in Afghanistan but was later told it was friendly fire—the military also reworked its death investigation procedures.

One of the biggest changes came in 2007 after a dead soldier's father complained that he didn't want his son flown home in the cargo hold of a commercial airline. Following an act of Congress, the Department of Defense began using chartered jets as a rule despite the added expense.

After watching the effect of public airport honors on the airline passengers, Major Beck initially had mixed feelings about the new process.

"The unintended consequence is a further detachment of the populace not seeing their fallen service member come home," he said. "I think that in many ways the people in this country are detached from the war—financially detached, emotionally detached. With the exception of their political stance—that's how they're attached—is what party they belong to. That young lance corporal, his politics don't mean anything. He's fighting for the guy next to him and for us."

On that subject his views often boil over.

"We consider these men and women who go forward to fight for us the lifeblood of our country, national treasures. When we lose something, we lose something important, and we should feel it. If you don't feel this loss in some way, I'm not so sure you're an American, frankly," he said. "When I hand that flag to them and say, 'On behalf of a grateful nation,' it's supposed to mean something. If [the public] is emotionally detached in some way, I don't know how grateful they really are. Politics aside, is the nation grateful for that loss? If they're emotionally detached, it's almost— It's almost criminal."

Major Beck has also personally witnessed missteps, such as the time a chaplain, confronted by a distraught mother cursing the president, told the woman there was no need for that kind of language.

Major Beck pulled the chaplain aside and told him the mother could say whatever she wanted.

"I think it caught him off guard. I don't know what his thoughts are on the war—I don't particularly care. But in that environment, his thoughts on the war don't matter. Defending the president is not our role at that moment. The president doesn't need our defense—particularly in that moment. The families need us. What that moment calls for is for us to be compassionate, empathetic, and to try to understand where they are and how to navigate this. That's what's important, and politics has no room there. The best way to handle that situation is not to tell someone what they can or cannot do in their own home."

Also at the beginning of 2007 the Marine Corps instituted a notification policy similar to the Army's—that no knocks come between the hours of midnight and 5:00 A.M. Major Beck says he understands the rationale, but he also questions the decision's ultimate result.

"I'm not real set on this one. I just follow my instincts as a CACO [casualty assistance calls officer], which says that sleep is overrated when it comes to the death of a loved one," he said. "My instincts would be to instead mandate that the chaplain services are available to our CACOs at all hours of the day and night. Period. End of story. God and the Marines serve day and night, so, too, should our chaplains. Not that some don't, it's just not a standard of excellence across the country. . . ."

Then he thought back to that porch in Wyoming, after midnight, in the snow.

"Wouldn't you want to know as soon as you possibly could?" he asked. "If it was your son, would you want us to let you sleep?"

Many problems could be solved, Major Beck said, if everyone followed a simple principle: "To do this right, to do it properly, you have to look at these women as if they were your mother or your wife, and these men as if they were your father or your brother. And you have to ask, 'What would I want someone to do if it were me?' "

The commitment starts when the door opens. It never really ends.

"If you're going to pass on a message with that kind of power, don't you think that all your actions that follow should be equal to it?" he said. "Don't you think so?"

26

The Cost

MELISSA GIVENS WAS still numb when the man in an Army dress uniform handed her the check.

"They gave me six thousand dollars," she said. "All I wanted was my husband back."

The money arrived in May 2003 as Melissa, eight months pregnant, was still absorbing the news that the Army had delivered the day before.

That night as she lay awake, the worries came in waves: She was alone but also had to prepare for the new baby and care for his five-year-old brother. She knew her husband carried life insurance, but she had no idea how long it would last. She had no job. She knew nothing about financial planning.

Then she would think of Jesse again.

"Your brain is so messed up at the time. I can't think of what I'm doing. I'm not thinking of long-term goals, I'm just thinking of making it through today," she said. "But I have to think of my children's future."

The government benefits started with the $6,000 check, a tradition the military calls the "death gratuity." The payment to fallen troops' families, which is paid within days of notification, dates back nearly a century but had increased only modestly since then.

That changed dramatically in 2006 with the passage of a bill that increased the death gratuity payment to $100,000 and the maximum life insurance from $250,000 to $400,000. For each service member killed in the line of duty, the government pays up to $500,000 to survivors. Payments were made retroactive to October 7, 2001, to include troops killed in the wars in Afghanistan and Iraq.

For Melissa and many other survivors of troops killed in action, the money ended a long, stressful struggle over the same complicated, delicate question: How much is enough money to compensate military families for the ultimate sacrifice?

It was a question Jesse Givens worried about in that prescient journal entry he wrote before leaving:

If we are involved in combat and I fall, who will raise my children? Who will be there for my wife? I sacrifice not only my life, but a husband and a father's life also. Who will see that my wife can support my children through all of their years? Who will provide my family with their basic needs?

"You don't want to feel greedy," Melissa said. "You think, 'This isn't welfare—you owe us to take care of our kids because their father died for you.' But you feel like you're begging for it. I hate to think I'm begging for it. I have more pride than that."

The insurance money allowed Melissa to buy a house and a car, and to invest for her children's future. Occasionally, she convinces herself that it's okay to spend the money on things her husband would have bought had he survived—toys for the boys or a ring for her birthday. Still, she says, that only reminds her of what's missing the most.

"Sometimes you think, 'That's blood money,' " she said. "It's only here because he's not."

The death gratuity began in 1908 as a way to help survivors pay for immediate expenses through a lump-sum payment that amounted to six months of the service member's pay. Over the next century and several wars, the payment hardly increased. From 1956 to 1991 the maximum payment was $3,000. At the start of the Persian Gulf War, the payment was bumped to $6,000, half of which was taxable income. After troops began dying in the latest war in Iraq, the amount was raised to more than $12,000—this time tax-free.

While the death gratuity is meant to pay for immediate expenses such as flying relatives in for the funeral or taking time off work, all active-duty service members also carry a military life insurance policy worth much more.

The policies, first offered in 1965 with a maximum payout of $10,000, now carry coverage of up to $400,000. Service members are automatically enrolled for the maximum amount—which requires monthly premium payments of about \$26—unless they specifically decline it.

Since half of the troops serving overseas are not married, many military death benefit packages go to parents who must bury their sons and daughters. Many continue to search for innovative ways to keep their children's memories alive. They have established scholarships, built memorials, and created programs that help troops overseas. Others have sent supplies to Iraqi children.

For young war widows the needs are often more immediate: bills that don't stop, children acting up, and hours spent wading through reams of bureaucratic paperwork. At the same time they must remain wary of con artists attempting to prey on them for the life insurance money.

At her home in Arlington, Virginia, seventy-six-year-old Rose Lee regularly switches on her computer and relives the problems of the nation's newest war widows. As the legislation chair of Gold Star Wives of America, the self-described "old widow" monitors a special Internet chat room open only to new widows. There they find support and share stories of the problems that come with suddenly having so much money or no money at all.

"One of our young widows said her husband failed to put her and her children on the insurance—maybe he forgot to change it after he got married—so it went to the soldier's mother," Lee said. "She said the soldier's mother has no contact with the grandchildren because she didn't want to share the money with the mother and children."

Then there are the bureaucratic hoops that none of them could have foreseen.

"One lady was pregnant when her husband died," Mrs. Lee said, "and [government workers] actually asked, 'How do we really know this child is his?'"

Sometimes a simple trip to the doctor forces a new widow to retell her husband's story because after a service member is killed, he's classified as "retired."

Mrs. Lee recalled the story of one woman who applied for military benefits only to be told, "You're too young to be retired," leaving her to tell the painful story once again that her husband was killed in action.

Advocacy groups are many widows' only link to news and advice. After her husband's death, Melissa relied on news from an Army casualty assistance officer but lost touch when he was transferred. Although the military offers financial counseling services, Givens ended up working through her family.

"I'm so leery about trusting people. When it's gone, it's gone, and I don't have enough experience to get a job that can take care of us," she said of herself and her children. "That's the biggest thing—to take care of them. I just want to give them what he wanted."

In their home the boy Jesse Givens never saw looked up with a full-faced, squinty-eyed grin. It matched the smile on the man whose face still looks over the family from pictures throughout the home.

"You want the daddy bankie?" she asked little Carson, lifting up one of the items she had splurged on: a big, soft blanket silk-screened with a photo of Jesse and ringed by the words *I love you.*

She unfolded the blanket and wrapped the toddler in the face of his father.

"Yeah," she said. "I think he would have liked it."

PART 4

AFTER THE WAR, STORIES

Doc kept saying to me, "Stay strong.
Stay with me, Sergeant Ed."
He said, "You're not going to die on me." I told him, "You take
care of my babies." Doc Anderson said, "You're going to take
care of your babies. You're going to be just fine."

— SERGEANT GREGORY EDWARDS

27

Remembering the Brave

Aurora, Colorado

Jo AND BOB Burns searched the crowd in the baggage claim area, looking for someone else's son.

"That one over there with the military haircut," she said, nodding toward a young man. "Is that one of them?"

"I'm not sure," her husband said.

For the past several weeks they had tried to prepare for this day. They were supposed to come here to welcome their son home. Instead, they made the drive from Laramie—the same drive that Major Beck had made nearly a year earlier—to meet the young men who last saw their son alive.

"This has really upset me tremendously, thinking about these guys coming," Jo Burns said. "At the same time I think we need this."

During the drive to Denver, Bob said his mind drifted back to a night marked by a scream that still haunts him—the scream from his wife when she saw Major Beck at their door.

"The scream. I don't know how to describe it," he said. "Bone-chilling, bloodcurdling."

As he drove on, he felt his stomach sink all over again. He wondered if he could relive it all.

Inside the airport, as they waited to pick up Marines they had never met, Jo Burns wondered what the guys from Red Platoon would think of meeting their dead friend's mother.

"I think they probably feel guilty that they get to come home and he didn't," she said. "I don't want them to feel guilty. But on the other hand, I also wish it was my kid who got to come home. I'm glad they get to come home, but . . ."

She stopped the sentence with a thin white handkerchief printed with the Marines logo, one that had already absorbed nearly six months of tears.

Over the next twenty-four hours, Marines from around the country would fly to Denver to honor fallen friends and comfort their families during a ceremony called Remembering the Brave, organized by Major Beck. In the process, the servicemen were about to learn a lesson of their own: The families of the dead weren't the only ones who needed help to heal.

Near the baggage claim, Jo Burns finally spotted them: five tall young men, two wearing cowboy hats and all carrying telltale olive-drab bags stitched with the Marines emblem. She and her husband hurried toward them.

"Hi, guys," Jo Burns finally said, tentatively grasping the hand of the first one in line and then drawing him close, raising on her tiptoes for a hug. She then moved quietly down the line, looking up into their eyes as hers welled once again.

A few minutes later, as they headed to the hotel, she managed a smile.

"They hugged me back," she said, still sniffling. "I wasn't sure how apprehensive they would be, but that felt good. They hugged me back."

AMONG THE FAMILIES that gathered in the nearby airport hotel for the ceremony, one woman searched for the man she once formally addressed as Major Beck but had since learned to call Steve.

In 2004, Major Beck had knocked on Betty Welke's door in Rapid City, bringing the news that began a relationship that would stretch far beyond South Dakota.

Within days of the death of Marine Lance Corporal Joe Welke, the Marines from Colorado braved a snowstorm and scrapped their Thanksgiving plans to serve at the funeral and continue to watch over the family.

"The governor and the politicians didn't make it to the funeral because it was so close to Thanksgiving," Betty Welke said. "I was thinking, 'I hope you don't have a SUPPORT OUR TROOPS yellow ribbon on the back of your car.'"

A few months later Major Beck and his Marines made another

trip to South Dakota for a different kind of memorial service. They conducted a formal ceremony at Joe's high school to retire his football jersey alongside a set of Marine dress blues and his combat utility uniform in the high school gymnasium.

At the end of the ceremony, Major Beck presented Betty with the cammies Joe had worn in Iraq. She held the uniform to her face, crying.

"She was crying into it pretty good. And for me that was kind of perfect," Major Beck said, "because his combat uniform from Iraq has her tears in it. Her tears are in those threads forever."

After speaking with other families whose casualty notification officers were hardly as caring, Betty asked Major Beck if there was any way he could help them.

After realizing that several Marines had posthumous medals due, Major Beck saw his chance. Posthumous medals often arrive in the mail in loose envelopes. For Major Beck and the Gold Star mother, that was far from acceptable.

The two have different opinions on the war. Betty has questioned the cost since the invasion of Fallujah. Despite the differences, their friendship remains strong, Betty said.

During one conversation, on the day that would have been Joe's twenty-first birthday, Betty asked the major to tell her what was really happening in Iraq. For the next hour Major Beck spoke passionately about scenes he said not enough people see: the Iraqi elections; the small, successful everyday missions; and the positive days he saw ahead for Iraq—turning points he said her son helped make possible. He explained how he believed it could take more than a decade until the military's sacrifices pay off. The American public, he said, would have to learn to be patient.

During his response, she remained quiet.

"But is it worth it?" she asked him finally. "Was it worth his life?"

He looked her in the eyes.

"Betty, with all you've been through, that's not something I can answer for you," Major Beck said. "That's something for you to decide."

THE DAY BEFORE the Remembering the Brave ceremony, the Burns family sat with the young men in their son's company—the same group they had met at the airport. Instead of flying directly home to their families from Iraq, Kyle's Marines instead chose to sit with the family of the man they considered a brother.

"Thank you for the package you sent," said twenty-one-year-old Corporal Dustin Barker, one of Kyle Burns's best friends in the platoon.

"Thank you for your letter," said Kyle Burns's father.

"I'm sorry I didn't have a chance to write more," Corporal Barker said.

As the group sat at the table, the Marines began filling in the blanks of Kyle Burns's life at Camp Pendleton and in Iraq. They told his parents how he liked to bodyboard off the coast of California and about the games they would play while drinking. They also knew exactly how he died in Fallujah on Veterans Day, 2004.

"You can ask us anything. We need to get it out. We've been holding it in for so long," Corporal Barker said. "That's why we're here."

A T FORT LOGAN National Cemetery, the grass over Kyle Burns's grave was starting to grow in but had yet to fully take root.

"When you're over there, there's no time to grieve," Corporal Barker said as he looked at his buddy's grave. "You worry that if you do, you'll get someone killed."

For Lance Corporal Mike Ball, the shock and reality were similar.

"I started to let the tears come," he said of seeing his friend die, "but we had patrol in ten minutes. You have to shut it off. We just got in the vehicles and started driving."

Since then he has kept the grief somewhere else, a place in his mind he had yet to unlock.

"That night when I got back, I actually tried to get back to that place, I tried to mourn. But it was gone," he said. "And I knew I'd have to wait."

At the cemetery one of Kyle's high school friends began to ask the questions everyone had dodged—questions that arose from rumors and miscommunication, questions that only raised more questions.

"So, it was an AK-47 that hit him?" Kyle's friend asked.

"No, it was an RPG [rocket-propelled grenade]," Corporal Barker told him. "That's why I'm here. Sometimes things get mixed up."

"I heard that he lived long enough for them to give him last rites," Kyle's friend said.

"No," Corporal Barker said quietly. "It was very quick."

Over and over throughout the weekend, the Marines would repeat the story of the assault—not only Corporal Barker but the company commander, the corpsman who treated Kyle and Paul Webber, the platoon leader who was shoulder to shoulder with Kyle when he was killed and whose emotions spilled in the touching e-mails to his fiancée.

They told the story without embellishment or melodrama. There was no need for it, they said. Because of Kyle Burns's actions, they said, other Marines are still alive, and what more do you need?

"What were his last words?" someone asked.

"'I'm hit,'" Corporal Barker said.

For the Marines, repeating the story is part of their therapy.

"You'll tell the story a couple of times and you're all right, and then the third time, man, it just hits you again," Barker said.

Despite the pain, it is a story they will continue to tell.

"I'm going to be telling my kids and grandkids about these guys," Corporal Ball said. "My grandkids are going to be so sick of hearing about Burns . . . and Staff Sergeant Holder. They'll be saying, 'But Grandpa, we already heard that one.' And I'll say, 'You need to hear it again.' "

B EFORE THE EVENT began, Major Beck stood in the empty ballroom looking at a line of medals on the table and struggled with all they reflected.

"When you think about what these guys did, it's not easy to look at these medals," he said. "What's the trade-off? What's the exchange? How do you say, 'This is for your son.' "

As the man who stood on the doorsteps of the families of those fallen Marines, he understands how delicate he needed to be. He also knew how heavy the medals can weigh.

"It's not a trade, but in the minds of the mothers, I wonder if they think it is a trade and they're thinking, 'I don't want this medal. I want my son.' The only way I can dispel that is through something like this—by showing them the honor, by honoring their son."

Major Beck began planning the event after he heard about the number of posthumous medals due to the Marines whose families he watched over.

After attending so many funerals and crying with so many families he now considers his own, Beck decided they deserved better. Still, he said, some people continued to wonder if it was too much.

"Even some of our Marines say, 'Why are we doing this to the families? Why do you have to keep reminding them?'"

Major Beck shook his head.

"This isn't about reminding them. They don't need reminding. These families think about this every day of their lives."

He looked up, addressing every person who hasn't felt what those families have.

"This isn't about reminding them," he said. "This is about re-minding *you*."

ONCE THE LIGHTS dimmed in the ballroom, more than five hundred people fell silent.

"You are about to hear the descriptions of individual acts of courage," Major Beck said. "Listen closely. Listen. Closely."

For nearly an hour they heard detailed accounts of rocket-propelled grenades and improvised explosive devices, of ambushes and assaults, each with the same ending.

Slowly and methodically the Marines brought out the medals and citations, and knelt before a mother or father they had first met on the doorstep. Halfway through the ceremony First Lieutenant Paul Webber—the man who was with Kyle Burns when the twenty-year-old died, the man who worried for so long about the blood on his hands—moved forward.

A few hours earlier, First Lieutenant Webber had sat with the

Burns family, telling them everything he knew about what had happened. Without prompting, Jo Burns told him she knew he did everything he could and that she hoped he had no guilt.

"I think everyone feels some sense of guilt," he told her. "But it's something we're working through. I don't think it will ever go away completely. I had a real hard time with this—a *real* hard time."

That night in the silent ballroom First Lieutenant Webber held high the Navy and Marine Corps Commendation Medal with a combat "V" for valor. Then he knelt before the family.

After presenting Jo Burns with the medal, he brought out a pair of dog tags they all thought were lost.

"Oh! Oh!" she said through splitting cries. "Oh! Thank you!"

As the families reeled, the citations continued. For each family the Marines also presented a vase of yellow roses, one rose for each year of the dead Marine's life.

WHEN IT WAS all over, the two tallest, toughest-looking Marines at the Burns table stood and hugged Jo Burns and then hugged each other.

Suddenly, Lance Corporal Ball's face turned red and finally flooded. As he pressed his head into his buddy's shoulder, the sobbing spread. Other Marines from the company grabbed hold of each other. They held tight for nearly a minute, holding nothing back.

Finally, someone started to laugh. They all laughed for a few seconds and then went back to crying. They thumped one another on the back.

"That stuff has been bottled up for so long," Lance Corporal Ball said. "It feels so good to get it out. Now we can mourn, too."

28

Melissa, Dakota, and Carson Givens

M ARCH 11, 2005, was not Jesse Givens's thirty-sixth birth-day. Still, the party began in a home he never lived in, underneath portraits of the stoic soldier and smiling father that hang from nearly every wall. Family and friends grabbed black markers and started the afternoon by scrawling messages on the birthday balloons.

"We're going to send the balloons to heaven," Melissa said.

"So my dad can read them there," added seven-year-old Dakota.

I love you, Daddy, she wrote for the boy.

We love you, she wrote for little Carson.

Then she wrote her own message: *Another year. I still miss you like crazy. I hope your birthday is great. Love, Me.* In the kitchen she picked up candles in the shape of a 3 and a 6.

"It's hard to go from 'He's gonna be thirty-six' to 'He would have been thirty-six'. He would have been," she said, shaking her head. "It's hard to stay in denial when you talk about death in the past tense. And denial is a pretty good place to be. I tell myself it's been nearly two years. I should be over this now. I should be further than I am. I should be better. People say I look fine. I must fake it pretty well."

She placed the candles on the cake and carried it to the table.

"I like to think that he's somewhere watching over us," she said. "There are times when I actually believe that."

Last Friday afternoon in the dining room, they all sang the song that ended with "Happy birthday, dear Daddy. Happy birthday to you."

Then two little boys stood before the burning candles on the cake. Dakota took a deep breath, made a secret wish, and blew.

IN THE BEIGE tract-home neighborhood near Fort Carson army base, the soldiers in ruddy desert camouflage uniforms almost blended in. To Melissa they still stood out. Weeks earlier more than five thousand of them had left for their second major deployment to Iraq. They would be gone for at least another year. The departure brought Melissa another round of suppressed guilt.

"This may sound bad, but in a way I'm glad they're leaving," she said quietly.

"I don't want them to get hurt. I really don't want them to go back over, but in a sense I do want them to leave. I feel terrible about it, but I'll feel better when they're gone. I won't have to see the soldiers everywhere, and all those happy damn couples."

While the soldiers were away on the first deployment, it was easier to pretend that her husband was deployed with them.

"As I said, denial is a pretty good place to be," she said.

When they returned, however, so did reality. There were parades, flags flying from every home, tearful reunions, and the men in fatigues all around the neighborhood.

At the height of it all, Dakota asked if they could also hang a WELCOME HOME sign on their garage door.

"I told him no," Melissa said, "because I don't want Dakota to think in the back of his mind that his dad is coming home.

"He said, 'Well, let's hang the sign for the neighbors.' I said, 'No, let's not hang anything on our house.'"

Earlier in the day, as she drove to pick up the birthday cake, a miniature flag dangled from the rearview mirror. The flag was stitched with a single gold star. Melissa said she was content to hang the star in her car instead of her home.

"Safety reasons," she said, noting that these days hanging the gold star flag only advertises that it's likely a house where a woman lives alone.

As she drove to pick up the cake, she promised Carson to stop for hamburgers, triggering another regret. "I always used to give Jesse shit for his cholesterol," she said. "Now I think, why didn't I just let him have that hamburger? It wasn't going to kill him."

Once inside Wal-Mart she picked up the cake and headed to grab some toys for the boys. Since they couldn't buy any presents for Jesse, she decided to buy the gifts he might have purchased for his sons.

"I always tell Dakota, 'Your daddy came to me in my dreams and asked me to get this for you.'"

In the store she headed to the G.I. Joe section. In the closest Wal-Mart to the post, the aisle mirrored Fort Carson: Half of the toy soldiers were missing.

"They never can keep them in stock," Melissa said.

NEARLY TWO YEARS since the men in green uniforms showed up at the door, Melissa still hadn't gone through everything left behind. The family was about to move when Jesse was deployed, and many of his things remained in boxes. A few weeks earlier, she found a bag of dirty laundry that made her cry.

"We did all the laundry before he died, so none of his clothes smelled like him," she said. "Then I found this bag that hadn't been washed, and I just held the clothes up and smelled him. Guys all smell the same when they're clean, but when they're sweaty . . . I miss the way he stinks."

Similar reminders are everywhere.

"When I'm going shopping, I still buy food for him," she said. "Those jalapeño poppers, the ones with cheese in them. I hate those things, but he loved them. I'll come home, open up the groceries, and they're there. I'll put them in the freezer for a few months, until I realize nobody's going to eat them."

For a while she attended a support group for war widows, but she quit going months ago; the group eventually fizzled.

"Death was all we had in common," she said. "You're a grieving widow at home, and you're trying to deal with it all. So then when you only have a couple of good days a week, you don't want to spend them with someone shoving 'You're a grieving widow' in your face."

She has read the grief books and has regularly seen the chaplain at Fort Carson for private counseling, but mostly she says she has tried to get back to life on her own terms, trying to figure out what seems the most normal. Owing to a conversation she had with Jesse before he died, she even briefly tried dating. It didn't work out.

"Jesse told me before he left that he knew I didn't like to be alone and that if anything happened, he'd send someone," she said. "It's hard because I'm still in love with him."

That much is apparent to anyone who walks into the home, where they are greeted by the photos of Jesse on the walls along with the telltale triangular flag, his medals, and an honorary sword.

"I've got the saber, the flag, the urn, the shrine . . . I wonder how much is too much," she said. "I think, 'Is this normal? Or is it getting creepy?'"

On her computer, late at night, she continued to type:

Jesse, Jesse,

Hi baby I am missing you so bad again. Not sure why but when the nights start to turn colder my heart starts to hurt so bad. Sometimes I feel I may go crazy without you here. I start to wonder if it will always be this way? 10 years from now will I still feel like this? I don't think I have ever wanted anything so badly. Or wished for something so much. If you could just come home and make my heart better. We went to a memorial dedication for the Ft. Carson soldiers killed over this last year. That was so hard. I did pretty good considering they played TAPS while they read the over one hundred names. I was standing close to some of the families. It broke my heart to hear the mothers crying for their sons whom they would never see again. I thought again of your mother and the pain she must go through. We are all going through it but it is different for each of us. Carson went up to the rock afterwards and said bye bye Daddy, bye bye GI Joe. That is what he calls you now. It is very cute, very sad but still cute. With all the spooky stuff coming out for Halloween he started saying daddy dead monster, I told him no, daddy died and went to heaven, he is not a monster. So now he will say Daddy in heaven. I smile as my heart breaks and say yes that is where daddy is. The other day he told me you were in the water. I am still not sure where he got that one. Hopefully you are with him in some way that I don't know about. And that is why he says things like that. He is talking so good if you were here you would crack up at the way he says things. He acts a lot like you. He still has your beautiful eyes. I want to hold on to him so tight, holding on to him so that I can hold on to you. I try so hard to make him know you. I wear dog tags with your picture on them. He will kiss you then hold them up to my lips so that I can kiss you as well. When he sees American flags he thinks of you and says daddy flag. He is a mommy's boy, and he likes shoes lol I would say that is a lot like you. He walks around showing everyone his shoes. He tells them look nice shoes. It cracks me up. Maybe I will find him some with flames on them. He really lights up my world Jess, thank you so much for giving him to me. Dakota is doing pretty good, he is the best helper I could ever have. He helps take care of Carson and is the best big brother. You would be so proud of him. He talks to Carson about you. And still prays for you. He is doing a little better in school this year. He is still in scouts and plays soccer as well. I can't get him to clean his room for nothing though. I wish you were here to help me with him. You were so much better with him than I could ever be. He listened to you cause he always wanted to please you. He still is your boy. The biggest daddy's boy I have ever seen. Carson always wants to watch The Nightmare Before Christmas and Dakota says oh no not again, I have to laugh because I remember all the times I had to watch it with the 2 of you. Carson will try to sing the songs and Kota just rolls his eyes. I guess I will go now baby I need to get to bed. I just wanted to say I love and miss you and let you know how the kids are. Please watch over them and let them know you are still here in some way. I love you and my heart still breaks for you everyday. Goodnight my love. Love your angel

Missy

On his last Valentine's Day, the same day he received his orders to go to war, Jesse Givens recorded a message and placed it inside a teddy bear for the Bean. When Carson squeezes the teddy bear, he hears his father's voice:

Baby Bean, I haven't even seen you yet, but in my mind I've pictured you a million times. And I know you're a beautiful baby and I love you with all my heart. I'll be home s—

"It cut off before he finished," Melissa said.

As Carson grows, each milestone is intertwined with the father who wasn't there.

"When Carson turned one, I knew Jesse was gone for thirteen months; when Carson was twenty months old, I knew Jesse had been gone for twenty-one . . ."

She no longer calls the baby Bean. His nickname is Jesse's Baby, as in "Jesse's baby looks hungry. . . . Jesse's baby is grumpy, and Jesse should be here to take care of him. . . ."

On that last Valentine's Day, Jesse also recorded a message for the son he did know:

Don't let the crocodile or the fuzzy butt-tickling monkey get you. Say your prayers and dream about us in the park. I love you Toad and I'll be home soon.

Dakota shied away from the bear at first.

"He didn't like the bear because he said his daddy lied," she said. "[Dakota] said, 'He's not coming home soon.' "

FOR MONTHS AFTER Jesse's death that is all Melissa could think about—his death.

"For so long I focused on how he died, the way he died," she said.

After the tank crew returned from Iraq, she asked them to tell her everything. She learned how the tank fell into the canal as U.S. troops tried to quell fires set by insurgents, and how they tried in vain to rescue Jesse. It wasn't enough. Eventually, she asked to see the place where he died.

One day they agreed to let her inside the tank, which had returned from Iraq with the troops. The tank was painted with the nickname HOME SWEET HOME.

"I went inside, and they closed the hatch," she said. "I just sat there thinking, 'This is such a little hole. And he's so much bigger than me.' I just kept thinking, 'This is where he died. This little hole is where he died.'

"One of the other guys had told me about scratch marks. I tried not to look, but I couldn't stop thinking about him trying to scratch his way out and imagining what it was like as the tank filled with water. You take that last breath, and you can only hold it for so long before you have to breathe again. And all there is is dirty water. . . ."

The tank was eventually redeployed to Iraq, which doesn't bother her; she says she no longer thinks about it. In a way, she says, forcing herself to relive her husband's last moments helped her get past them.

"I used to only dwell on his death," she said. "Now I like to think more of the daddy and husband part of him instead of the dead soldier part. Because he was so much more. And after I understood that, that's when I could go on."

As the sun set on the birthday party, the family prepared to go outside and release the balloons to the man who wasn't there. Before that happened, though, Melissa had one last message to write:

> *Happy Birthday my love. I hope you know how much I love you and life is not the same without you. Please be proud of me. I am doing my best. I will never forget our time. Know that you are in my heart forever. Love, your wife, Missy.*

Outside, they released the balloons one by one.

"If a balloon pops, that means an angel grabbed it," Dakota said as they watched the colorful dots drift away into the dusk.

"That means we love him," Melissa said as the last balloon drifted from sight. "No matter where he's at right now, he knows we love him."

Later that evening, long after the leftover cake was put away and the wrapping paper trashed, Dakota lay on the floor, thinking back to the moment before he blew out the candles, and his wish.

"I wished that my dad could come back," he said softly and then looked over at his brother, who was playing happily with his new action figures. "I think that Carson probably just wished for more toys, so Carson already got his wish," Dakota said. "I know mine won't come true."

29

Navy Corpsman HM3 Christopher "Doc" Anderson

Walter Reed Army Medical Center, Washington, D.C.

ONE WEEK BEFORE Christopher "Doc" Anderson's funeral, a sergeant with no legs sat outside Walter Reed Army Medical Center and closed his eyes.

"You're going to have to give me a minute here," he said.

For weeks Sergeant Gregory Edwards couldn't tell the story of what happened on October 21, 2006. He lied when asked about it, saying he couldn't remember anything. The problem was he could remember almost everything.

On that day, he said, his patrol stopped in front of a house owned by a government official in Ramadi. The sergeant stepped on what he thinks was a mine or a radio-controlled explosive.

"I was unconscious, and when I woke up, the first face I saw was Doc Anderson," Sergeant Edwards recounted. "He said, 'Don't worry about it, Sergeant. It's not that bad.'"

The sergeant looked up and saw his legs or what little was left of them. He saw the blood, looked at his mangled hand, and went into shock.

"Doc kept saying to me, 'Stay strong. Stay with me, Sergeant Ed.' He said, 'You're not going to die on me.'"

The Marines carried Sergeant Edwards into an Iraqi home where Doc Anderson began emergency first aid.

"I told him, 'You take care of my babies.' Doc Anderson said, 'You're going to take care of your babies. You're going to be just fine.' There was a lot of pain and . . . and . . ."

The sergeant stopped and closed his eyes again.

"Give me a minute," he said.

They sped in the Humvee to the nearest aid station. Anderson tied tourniquets with one hand while elevating the sergeant's head with the other. Then Doc Anderson started shouting at his patient.

"I could feel myself slipping away, wanting to go to sleep, and Doc started yelling at me," Sergeant Edwards said. "I was ready to enter whatever afterlife there is, and he kept yelling at me, telling me it was going to be okay."

Doc Anderson later would tell his friends and parents that it was the most terrifying day of his life, that he constantly second-guessed himself, wondering if he had done everything he could have and should have. He told his closest friends that he had lost the sergeant's pulse three times on the way to the clinic but that each time he had managed to bring him back. More than thirty days later, Sergeant Edwards woke up at Walter Reed. He remembered one voice:

"The last thing I heard was Doc saying, 'You're going to be okay.'"

Before being deployed, Navy corpsmen say, they have a choice to "go blue," serving their time on a ship or stateside, or to "go green," assigned to the Marines. Doc Anderson volunteered to go green.

Before arriving in Iraq in early September, Christopher was assigned to Alpha Company of the First Battalion, Sixth Marine Regiment, a group with a decorated history dating to World War I. The rookie corpsman was soon on the front with the infantry, tasked with securing some of the most dangerous neighborhoods in Iraq.

Before the Marines headed to Ramadi, they had to know that the sailor from Colorado with the massive pack of medical gear was the kind of man they could trust with their lives.

A traditional saying holds that a Marine infantryman doesn't wonder if his corpsman will save his life, he wonders when.

"When you get a new corpsman, he has to prove himself, that he can do the same things the Marines can do," Sergeant Edwards said. "When we do PT [physical training], he has to keep up. When we go on our hikes, he has to carry the same gear plus his medical gear, which must weigh an additional thirty pounds. And he can't fall back."

A fourth-generation sailor, Doc Anderson never fell back.

Although he was relatively scrawny, it didn't take long for the corpsman to prove that he could run as quickly and last as long as any of the "grunts." He used his height to help shorter guys over walls and fences, following behind, always looking out for them.

Using his medical equipment as a universal translator and icebreaker, he treated Iraqis as well as his own men, forging trust in a place where the word is elusive. If he saw an Iraqi child with a cut or scrape, he would treat the child with antibacterial cream and bandages in an attempt to win his part of the war with Band-Aids.

He earned frequent smiles from the Marines, often at his own expense. He was teased endlessly for his trademark bouncy walk— a literal spring in his step which he swore he didn't do on purpose. He banked an endless reserve of bad jokes, the punch lines of which he would laugh at much too loud and much too long, until everyone around was laughing both with him and at him.

"I like to remember the good times with Doc," Sergeant Edwards said. "Sometimes he was a complete jackass."

I N H I S H O M E office in Colorado, Rick Anderson loaded a DVD into his computer, pressed Play, and the memorial started again.

The video was taken somewhere in Iraq after Doc's death. On the screen a group of Marines from Alpha Company gathered near two "field crosses"—sets of empty boots split by a rifle and topped with a combat helmet, the symbol of a fallen service member.

One Marine approached a makeshift podium and began to speak. "Men, we gather this evening to honor the service, commitment, and friendship we've all come to know and share with our fallen brothers here tonight. Lance Corporal Thomas Echols and HN Christopher Anderson," the unidentified Marine said.

Echols, a twenty-year-old Marine from Kentucky, was killed in the same battle that claimed Doc Anderson's life.

"I say brothers because they are brothers," the Marine continued. "They're brothers based on the same hardships that create a very special bond between Marines and sailors, quite honestly, like no other I've come to know. I don't think you can really understand that bond, that brotherhood, unless you're standing here with us—unless you're facing the same hardships, the same dangers, day in and day out."

At the end of the video, the members of Doc's squad gathered to send a message to his family.

"Mr. and Mrs. Anderson . . . he was a brother to all of us, loved by us all," one said.

"He saved my best friend's life," said another, referring to Sergeant Edwards.

"I want you to know that your son was awesome, and every day we went on patrol, we had his back, and we still do," said another.

"He was my best friend out here. He was my combat buddy," said another. "I think about him every day when I get up, and as I get ready to leave that wire [into the combat zone], he's with me.

My prayers go out to you, his family, and I want you to know that his family here misses him more than anything in the world. We miss him, we love him, and welcome to our family."

As the men voiced their concern for the family, Rick Anderson said he worried about them.

"I'm thinking this guy had to regroup, grab his weapon, and go back at it," he said after watching the DVD. "When I think I'm having a bad day, I think about the guys who had to go back out there. The young men with my son had to go right back to work."

"We get to come home and cry," Debra Anderson said. "They have to go back to work."

On the DVD, at the end of the funeral service each man walked to the field crosses. As they walked past, each man saluted.

The last Marines in line kissed Doc's empty helmet.

INSIDE WARD 58 at Walter Reed Army Medical Center, the sergeant shook out a Marlboro Red. These days, despite doctor's orders, even his mother won't give him grief about smoking.

"I figure he survived that," Cheryl Edwards said, nodding toward his legs. "He can have a cigarette."

After thirty-six surgeries, much of the shrapnel remained inside. The sharp chunks of metal will work their way out during the next several years as his body expels the war.

Sergeant Edwards's left hand was shattered in the blast. The bones pulverized "like powder," he said. The hand is now a gnarled brown mess of dead, flaky skin and giant Frankenstein stitches that wrap around the fingers that have been reattached and secured with surgical pins. He can move his thumb and forefinger like a crab pincer, but he has lost some of his knuckles, so his other fingers are shorter than they were. At one point surgeons suggested amputating some fingers to save his hand.

"The doctor came in and said, 'How attached are you to that index finger?'" Sergeant Edwards said. "I told him, 'I'm attached to all my body parts. I've already lost enough.'"

The stumps of his legs are discolored patchwork quilts of skin grafts. One leg was rebuilt with the thigh muscle from a donor body; it now ends several inches above his knee. The other was amputated through the kneecap.

A bandage on his head covers a quarter-sized dark red hole, which otherwise remains framed in the "high and tight" Marine haircut.

Outside the hospital a man in a camouflage uniform paused at Sergeant Edwards's wheelchair and offered his hand in thanks.

"I get that a lot," he said after the man left, pulling out another cigarette. "But me, personally, I don't think I need to be thanked for my service. I chose this. I know that being blown up or dying is one of the hazards of my job. If you don't expect to get hurt as a Marine infantryman, you're in the wrong line of work."

This had been his third tour in Iraq. He went in on the initial invasion and saw the statue of Saddam Hussein fall. During his second tour, he was nearly electrocuted and spent time at Walter

Reed recovering. Although he is a living example of the war's cost, he prefers to look back on what he says will be lasting benefits of his sacrifice.

"I lost my legs, not for this country, but for the country of Iraq, so their children will be able to run around just like mine," he said as he watched his daughters, ages three and five, playing on the hospital grounds. "If time was turned back, I'd do it all over again."

He says he told President George W. Bush the same thing during a recent visit. Before leaving for Texas for Christmas vacation, the president and first lady made rounds at Walter Reed, speaking to many of the wounded.

Sergeant Edwards's mother said that the president, after visiting with Sergeant Edwards for about half an hour, spoke to other injured service members and then returned to the sergeant's room.

"[The president] said, 'Some of the guys have cussed me out. Some said they hated me. But I'm going to quote you word for word in my next speech,'" Cheryl Edwards said.

Outside Walter Reed, Sergeant Edwards's daughters ran back to him, and he boosted one of them into his lap. The girls call the stumps of his legs "Daddy's boo-boo."

BACK INSIDE WALTER Reed, Sergeant Edwards grimaced. He lives every minute with pain that would make most people wince. When his face contorts in pain during physical therapy, it nearly shakes the hospital table.

"I'm not a very good patient," he said. "I have no patience."

Nearby, men with new computerized legs ran on treadmills while others tried out their new arms. In a corner of the room, two little girls and a young boy watched *How the Grinch Stole Christmas*, oblivious to their parents' efforts to figure out their new limbs. When he first awoke in the hospital, Sergeant Edwards asked not to see his own two girls.

"It's not that I didn't want to see them," he said, "but I didn't want them to see me."

When told that his Doc died from a mortar attack, he asked his wife and kids to leave the room.

"My dad stayed with me," he said. "For two days I was heavily depressed. I was heavily medicated. It took me two days to cope with it without being medicated. Now that the funeral is close, I'm starting to have a hard time with it again."

Sometimes, while asleep, his arms will flail and his body will thrash with the inevitable nightmares, so family members take turns watching him, making sure someone is there to wake him from battle.

One week earlier, the commandant of the Marine Corps met with Sergeant Edwards at the National Naval Medical Center in Bethesda, Maryland. In the center of the lobby is an enormous bronze statue of a Navy hospital corpsman carrying a wounded Marine whose legs drag on the ground.

"I can't put it into words what a corpsman means to his Marines," he said. Then he thought back to that bronze memorial. "It says it all in that statue," he said. "It's called *The Unspoken Bond*."

· · ·

THE AMERICAN FLAG at Arlington National Cemetery flies at half-staff every weekday. An average of twenty-five funeral processions a day wind near it, past the white rows of marble where privates and unknown Civil War veterans lie near Medal of Honor winners and presidents. Arlington is where Memorial Day officially began, the place where it never ends.

The cemetery holds the remains of more than three hundred thousand men and women on more than six hundred acres. In Section 60, the place where they bury soldiers from the latest war, the headstones are fresh.

According to the Department of Defense, the cemetery recently acquired enough land to keep it available for burials until 2060; that is, if the current rate of burials holds.

Not far from the cemetery, the massive Iwo Jima Memorial towers over an intersection, honoring the Marines who raised the flag over Mount Suribachi during World War II. Although it is considered a Marine memorial, one of the men immortalized thirty-two feet tall in heavy bronze is John "Doc" Bradley, the unit's corpsman.

At the beginning of World War II, corpsmen and Army medics wore red crosses on their uniforms. That stopped when the enemy began using the crosses as targets, knowing that the servicemen would do anything to save their medics. These days the corpsmen wear the Marines' digital camouflage and carry full weaponry while in combat zones. Still, as the tombstones reflect, they remain primary targets. Since September. 11, 2001, Navy corpsmen have comprised more than one-third of all Navy casualties.

At Arlington, visitors can buy a $6 ticket for a "Tourmobile" that whisks them through the cemetery in thirty minutes, a tour that pauses at the eternal flame of President Kennedy, the Tomb of the Unknowns, and the home once owned by Robert E. Lee, back when the cemetery was a plantation.

The Tourmobile doesn't go near Section 60. Across the street, the ground is empty. Workers are preparing Section 61.

30

Marine Corporal
Brett Lee Lundstrom

Pine Ridge Indian Reservation, South Dakota

O N A FREEZING overcast night in the Badlands, a sun-bleached buffalo skull lay near the door of the small domed shelter supported by willow branches and covered by a heavy tarp. A Lakota Sioux man closed the flap on the door, leaving them all in darkness pierced only by the pulsing glow of orange rocks sprinkled with sage.

Clad only in a pair of shorts, Marlin Under Baggage poured water on the rocks, filling the sweat lodge with a pungent steamy heat that all of them could taste.

It started just after midnight with a nightmare that had already come true.

"Before Brett left for Iraq, he told me he had a dream that he was going to be shot," Marlin Under Baggage said. "He was scared.

He didn't think he was coming back. Still, he went. That is courage. That is bravery."

Ten months earlier, during the wake at Little Wound High School, the Lakota had welcomed Brett Lundstrom's body home. It was only the beginning.

In the Lakota tradition, mourning takes at least a year, as the spirit of the dead watches over those who grieve on its journey to the other side, where tradition holds that the dead will be reunited with the Lakota ancestors.

Every week since then, they came to the sweat lodge, to continue the journey for Corporal Lundstrom and for those left behind.

"He also worried about his little brother," Marlin Under Baggage said to the darkness. "He worried."

A few miles away, Brett Lundstrom's only sibling arrived on the reservation from his own tour in Iraq.

Inside the sweat lodge, the drumbeat began.

Steam enveloped the darkness, soaking the Lakota people, blasting them with air so hot that some bent over to breathe the cooler air near the dirt floor. As sweat dripped from their skin and drenched their hair, they prayed and smoked tobacco from a sacred pipe.

"I want to pray for Brett and for Eddy. I want to pray for the warriors," Glorianna Cordova said. "I also want to pray for all the Iraqi people who have died. All the children."

The prayers continued, followed by traditional Lakota songs — songs of healing, songs of purification. Nine months before, many of them stayed awake for forty-two hours straight during the wake for Brett Lundstrom. Now, as they welcomed home his brother, it neared 2:00 A.M.

"One more song," George Apple said as he picked up his drum. "I want to sing a song for the soldiers."

THE NEXT MORNING on the Pine Ridge reservation a soldier named *Wicahci Kailehya* awoke wrapped in his name.

"It can be translated as Shining Star or Fiery Star," Doyla Lundstrom said of her son's Indian name. "I like Fiery Star."

After Eddy's return from Iraq, his mother gave him a traditional native star quilt. On the quilt, yellow diamonds burst from a night-black sky.

"He loved it," she said. "When I woke him up this morning, he was wrapped in it."

Inside the Lakota Prairie Ranch Resort, the traditional drum circle began again.

Only three weeks after Eddy returned from Iraq, his family returned to the reservation to help dedicate a meeting room at the motel in Brett's honor. As they gathered around the dedication table, one of the reservation's enforcement rangers, Francis Jamie Big Crow, bowed his head. In 2003 he served as an escort for Lori Piestewa, the first woman killed in the war and the first female Native American to die in combat overseas in service to the U.S. military. Then in January he rode his horse in front of a clapboard wagon carrying the casket of Brett Lundstrom.

"It was a tremendously great honor to be on horseback—especially as a horse nation," he said. "Gosh, I can feel it right now, just saying this."

Inside Little Wound High School in nearby Kyle, they still keep the pictures of each reservation member who has served in Iraq and Afghanistan. A group of mothers has set up a support group. Now the fathers are starting to come, too. It is far from their only worry: The reservation also grapples with unemployment, alcoholism, and a methamphetamine problem that gnaws at the tribe from the inside out.

"Brett's death wasn't a tragedy. It was a huge loss, but it wasn't tragic," said Marlin Under Baggage, Brett's uncle. "Last weekend three young people lost their lives here—one in an accident, one in a stabbing, and one from an overdose. Those are the tragedies."

In a place only a few miles from the Wounded Knee massacre more than a century ago, many at Pine Ridge openly question the cost of the current war—in billions of dollars and lives lost—while still remembering the battles that left them on the reservation.

"You go back and look at acts of terrorism. This country committed the first act of terrorism—on the Lakota people, at Wounded Knee," Francis Jamie Big Crow said. "People say, 'Remember 9/11.' I wish they would also remember 1890, Wounded Knee, because Native American people were lost."

Still, they continue to serve. As they were holding the ceremony, more than sixty Lakota from Pine Ridge were overseas. A tribe member from Rosebud had recently returned after surviving a gunshot from a sniper.

"This is for all of the things all of them have done," Ed Lundstrom Sr. said of the room's dedication to his son. "Brett is the face of it, but this is for all of them. This is for all of the servicemen and -women."

The drum circle played a song written for Brett by a Denver-based drum group called Good Feather, the same group that played at his burial service at Fort Logan National Cemetery. *"Wanbli Isnala,"* the song is called, *"Lone Eagle."*

After the ceremony, Brett's great-uncle, Birgil Kills Straight, looked around the room. "It's not just four walls anymore," he said. "It seemed sterile to this point, and then it took on a life."

A few minutes later, Eddy and his best friend, Frankie Lugo, stepped outside for a cigarette.

"The songs," Lugo said, his eyes red. "That's what gets me every time, those songs. I wish I could understand the words. Did you understand it?" he asked Eddy.

The young soldier stared out at the brown hills. "I understood *'Wanbli Isnala.'"*

LATER THAT NIGHT, inside a Rapid City pizzeria more than an hour's drive from the reservation, Eddy looked up at the television screen at a commercial for *Flags of Our Fathers,* the movie about the Marines who hoisted the U.S. flag at Iwo Jima during World War II.

"I read the book. I really liked it," he said quietly. "It's sad what happened to the Indian, though."

Long before the book or the movie, almost everyone around here knew the story of Ira Hayes, a quiet, shy Pima Indian who helped raise the flag on Mount Suribachi. He returned home a hero, but he struggled with the attention. Hayes fell into alcoholism and died at thirty-two.

In the restaurant, Frankie Lugo watched as Eddy, his best friend, wound his way over. "Think of it. Every time he's introduced, people say, 'This is Eddy. He just got back from Iraq. His brother died over there,'" Lugo said. "I don't think he should have to be reminded all the damn time."

As the family prepared to leave the restaurant for a pool hall several blocks away, a snowstorm kicked up, and the family decided to drive. Eddy shook off the idea, insisting on walking through the storm.

"But you have to walk across a major road," Lugo said.

"I'm not afraid of a few cars," he said. "They don't blow up over here."

By the time the Lundstrom family made it into the smoky haze of the pool hall, Eddy was already there. He had a large bloody gash on the palm of his hand.

"I had to jump over a fence," he said. "It's no problem, though. All you have to do is cauterize the wound. In Iraq you have to do what you have to do." He took the cigarette from his mouth and mashed it into his palm, searing the wound without flinching. Then he stuck the cigarette back in his mouth.

Sometimes Eddy will order an extra beer and leave it on the counter without touching it. It is for his brother.

When people in the bar learned who Eddy is, which did not take long, they gathered around his table. When they found out that his new unit was scheduled to leave for Afghanistan within the next several months, their pride mixed with anger.

"Don't go back, man, don't go back," said Alfred Leftwich. "We can only lose one Lakota per family, only one."

"Somebody's gotta go," Eddy said.

He took a sip of his beer.

"Don't worry about me," he said. "I got an angel watching over my shoulder. Yeah, I got an angel on my shoulder."

31

Melissa, Dakota, and Carson Givens

Fountain, Colorado

THE TWO GIVENS boys stood next to each other in the basement, staring at a picture of a man that only one of them had a chance to meet.

"Who is this?" seven-year-old Dakota said.

"Da-da," nineteen-month-old Carson said.

"That's right," Dakota said. He then looked up. "At first, he called me Da-da, and I had to tell him, 'No, Da-da's dead. I'm Dakota, your brother.' "

From a steamer trunk in the basement—the place where his mother stored all the things the Army sent back from the war— Dakota picked out the colorful card that Jesse Givens had bought for the boy's birthday, intending to mail it from the war zone.

"He left it in his tank, and it drownded," Dakota said as he closed the card, which was still warped from the water. "It drownded with him."

The boy then closed the lid of the steamer and asked if anyone wanted to play video games or action figures. In the past year and a half, Dakota had become an expert at changing the subject. Up in his room, he immediately headed for his huge cache of toys.

Eventually, however, his little brother returned, changing the subject back as he dragged in a pillow silk-screened with his father's picture.

"Da-da, nigh-nigh," the toddler said.

"That's right," Dakota said. "Da-da, night-night."

WHEN SHE WATCHED her son playing alone in his room, Melissa Givens knew some of the things going on in his head. They were going on in hers, too.

"He's keeping a lot of it in," she said. "Sometimes he'll just start screaming or crying, and nothing will make him stop, and I'll say, 'Maybe this is a good time to talk about your dad.' "

Dakota's grades suffered to the point that he had to repeat kindergarten. He started seeing a therapist. Still, Melissa said, "It's hard to determine what [behavior] is from him trying to deal with this and what's perfectly normal. I've never had a seven-year-old before."

One of her biggest concerns is discipline, both for her son and for herself. "We'll be at the store, and he'll say, 'Mom, can I have this?' And if I say no, he'll say, 'Well, my daddy would have bought it for me.' If I'm in a certain mood, I'll give in."

At home she tried to fill in for Jesse, playing video games with Dakota and organizing make-believe light saber battles with both boys. Still, she says, she'll never master "the daddy thing."

"He always made time to go outside, to the park, to the mountains," she said. "I'm not into the outdoors."

In hopes of rekindling some of those excursions, Melissa enrolled Dakota in Cub Scouts and volunteered as a den mother. Since Jesse's death, the community largely reached out to the Givens family and others who had lost loved ones in the war, flooding their home with cards, gifts, and offers of support.

Then there is the other side.

"Remember when those girls said Dad got killed because he was a wuss?" Dakota asked his mom. "They said, 'I don't care if your dad is dead.' "

"I remember that," Melissa said. "You came in, and you said you wanted to hit them. But you didn't, and I was so proud."

She shook her head. "Little kids can be mean sometimes."

But so can adults, as she found out at a party for soldiers at Fort Carson.

"A couple of people were upset that I was at the Christmas party because I remind them of what can happen to their husband," she said. "I wanted to tell them, 'Look, your husband is not going to die if my kids play with your kids. Your husband is not going to die if I'm here.' "

So she decided to remain in Fountain, promising to continue to bring her kids to military events, for one simple reason:

"I just want people to remember [Jesse], and by talking about him, it shows the boys that their daddy's a hero. Dakota says he doesn't want his daddy to be a hero; he wants him to be a daddy. I just want them to remember. And I'm just going to be there to remind everybody that, hey, we're still here."

IN HIS ROOM, Dakota looked up at the first thing he sees each morning: the picture of his father on the wall.

"The park was my favorite," he said. "He would take me to the park whenever I wanted, and we'd play. He would chase me around, and then I would run, and then he would pop up, and then we would run all over and over."

Carson interrupted Dakota by trying to shove an animal cracker in his brother's mouth. Dakota pushed his brother away and then sat up on his bed.

"I'm going to do everything [with Carson] that my dad did with me," he said. "I'm going to take him to the park. I'm going to take him everywhere my dad took me. And if my mom dies, I'm going to take care of him like she takes care of me."

Dakota no longer curls up in the corners of the house to sleep, fighting off nightmares.

"But he still says he gets lonely," Melissa said. "Last night Dakota got up and went to sleep with his brother in the toddler bed. They need each other."

She rolled her eyes as the boys returned downstairs and started another wrestling match on the floor. Then she smiled.

"Dakota told me that his job is to tell Carson all about Dad. He said that's his main job, to tell his brother about Jesse," she said. "Then the other day he asked me, 'When is my job going to be over?' I said, 'Pretty much never, Kota. Pretty much never.'"

32

Katherine and Jimmy Cathey

Brighton, Colorado

On Christmas morning, 2005, Katherine Cathey woke up in a hospital bed in the maternity ward, looked at the crib, and saw her husband.

"That cowlick—he has the same cowlick on the right side of his head," she said of James J. Cathey Jr. "He has the nose. One of his ears sticks out more than the other, like his dad. He has these really long fingers and feet like Jim. And he smiles. He smiles a lot."

On her handmade calendar, the twenty-four-year-old war widow had marked all the things she had planned to send to Iraq that month: "congrats on baby card, baby pictures, cigars, candy."

Not long after Jim and Katherine married, doctors told the

couple that for medical reasons it was unlikely that Katherine would ever get pregnant. After she found out they were wrong, Jim sent her a Mother's Day card early, while he was training in the desert in California.

"I can't wait, baby!" he wrote.

After Jim deployed, Katherine would spend hours with her hands on her belly, talking to the baby about his father. Although he would never feel the baby kick, the Marine tried to remain as close as possible.

"Jim sent me an e-mail that he had this dream that he was holding the baby, but that it was really tiny, like he was able to hold it in his hand," she said. "The last time Jim was alive, the baby was so tiny."

Following an emergency cesarean section, "Jimmy" Cathey was born on December 22, 2005: seven pounds, ten ounces. After spending his first two days in the nursery, Jimmy was allowed to spend Christmas Eve in Katherine's room, their first night together.

Katherine and her parents arrived back home the next day to presents sent from around the country and around the world, from strangers who had learned their story. Among them, Katherine found a special gift from one of the men who had served with her husband in Iraq.

"I opened the box and just started crying. It was a tricycle. I could just picture him riding it when he was older," she said as the tears fell again. "And his dad wouldn't be there."

. . .

SINCE THE DAY the Marines showed up at Katherine's door, the periodic reminders of James Cathey's life and death seemed endless. It started the day Katherine returned from the funeral, walked to the mailbox, and found a letter her husband had sent only a few days before he died.

Soon afterward a care package was returned unopened. She had sent it two weeks before Jim's death. It sat on the counter for the next four months, until Katherine's mother finally asked if she could put it in a closet for safekeeping.

"It's hard to throw stuff away—even little notes I jotted down while he was still alive; I don't want to throw them away. I'm doing my best to save everything I can. I want to go through it with Jimmy. I hope he asks a lot about his dad," she said. "I'm sure he will."

She keeps his desert camouflage uniforms in a footlocker delivered from Iraq. At the bottom was the last shirt Katherine wore before Jim left. It still smelled like her perfume.

As the weeks wore on, Katherine began to expect the reminders from Iraq. She wondered what would arrive next. She never expected the call that came in late September 2005.

"Major Beck called the week before Jim's birthday," Katherine said. "He said, 'There's no easy way to say this. Remember how you checked the box that said you would like to be notified if more of Jim's body was found?' "

.   .   .

As she spoke with Major Beck, Katherine learned that morticians at Dover Air Force Base in Delaware had identified a leg that belonged to her husband. Although the situation is rare, the military says, it is not always possible to transport all the remains of a dead serviceman at once. Sometimes DNA testing is required first.

It was up to Katherine to decide the next step: She could leave the leg with the mortuary affairs team in Dover, she could have it cremated, or she could have it interred with her husband's body.

"He said, 'I'll give you some time. Do what you think is right.'"

The decision didn't take long.

"I decided I'd like to have part of him here with me."

For the Marines, transporting the ash-filled urn was no different from their original mission to bring Jim Cathey's body back to his family from Iraq. A Marine was required to escort the urn each step of the way.

At Katherine's request the Marines called upon Second Lieutenant Marcus Moyer who had trained with Jim Cathey in Quantico, Virginia.

"I never really looked at it as escorting a box or escorting ashes.

I treated it as though he was with me," Second Lieutenant Moyer said. "I never left it alone."

When crew members on the airplane to Denver discovered the Marine's mission, they asked to shake his hand. One flight attendant wrote him a heartfelt thank-you note on a United Airlines napkin.

"As we were coming into Denver, the pilot came on the loudspeaker and announced that we had a special passenger onboard," Second Lieutenant Moyer said.

The pilot then read the information about Jim Cathey and requested that passengers remain seated until the Marine left.

"As I was walking forward, people said things—'Oo-rah,' if they knew I was with the Marines, or 'Thank you,' or 'You're our hero.' Or they would clap. . . . Regardless of their feelings about the war, they all seemed very supportive. People would come up and thank me for my service. They would call me a hero."

The Marine paused for a long time.

"Whenever I could do it without crying, I would tell them that . . . that I wasn't the hero but that I knew a lot of them."

That night after Second Lieutenant Moyer met up with Major Beck, the Marines once again pulled up to Katherine Cathey's home, clad in their formal dress blue uniforms.

"It's another notification," Major Beck said. "Jim doesn't die all over again, but it's the introduction of more pain—and another whole difficult process we need to go through. And everything starts over. In a way, it was like walking up to that porch for the first time."

. . .

THE BRONZE BOX-SHAPED urn is emblazoned with the Marine Corps logo. Beneath it is an inscription:

2ND LT. JAMES J. CATHEY

OCTOBER 8, 1980–AUGUST 21, 2005

Katherine picked up the urn and sat cross-legged on her bed. Before he left for Iraq, the couple never talked about death.

"I remember in Lejeune trying to bring something up about it," Katherine said. "He just started crying and said, 'I don't want to think about it. You don't know how scared I am.' I think he had a feeling that he wasn't coming back."

When she is out in public, Katherine rarely brings up the story of her husband's death. She doesn't want to make others uncomfortable.

"Everyone says the same thing: 'I don't know what to say,'" she said. "I can't imagine being on the other side of it. I don't know what I'd say, either."

She stopped and thought.

"I guess I want them to say, 'Wow, what an amazing husband you had.'"

With the birth of her son, Katherine planned to move into her own home, with an area dedicated to her husband's memory. After that she planned to attend college and study anthropology—the same subject in which Jim Cathey earned his degree. She also plans to be buried eventually with her husband, along with his ashes.

"I kind of feel like I have part of him with me," she said. "And it may sound silly to some people, but since I've decided to have the urn buried with me, it will be like all of Jim will be back together once I am with him."

She placed the urn back on the shelf, near the baby's bassinet. On one side of the bronze box she had inscribed a quote from one of her favorite letters: *I am here for you even when I am not, and that's the way it will always be. Semper, Jim.*

THE SOFT GREEN baby blanket no longer smells like Second Lieutenant James J. Cathey.

"The night before he left for Iraq, I asked him to sleep with the blanket so that when the baby was born, he would know how his father smelled," Katherine said, holding up the blanket she knitted while her husband was stationed at Camp Lejeune, preparing to deploy.

"I can still see him there that night," she said. "He just held the blanket and slept with it. He went to sleep before I did, and I remember watching him, crying, thinking about how much I was going to miss him and that he wasn't going to be there when the baby was born."

She lifted the blanket, leaned into the bassinet, and wrapped it around her son.

"The blanket smells more like a baby now," she said softly, "but there's something about Jimmy that also smells like his dad."

She nuzzled her nose with the infant's.

"I don't know what it is, but I feel like he's an old soul," she said, staring into his eyes as he fell asleep. "There's just something about him that makes me think that he's already experienced a lot of life."

33

Navy Corpsman HM3 Christopher "Doc" Anderson

Arlington National Cemetery, Arlington, Virginia

THE SERGEANT WITH no legs sat inside the cemetery, thinking about how this homecoming was supposed to happen.

Sergeant Edwards had spent the past two months in a hospital bed, grimacing as he devised his own painful physical regimen to strengthen the tender stumps that end just above his knees, hoping to earn his prosthetic legs early. His unit, including the man who saved his life, wasn't supposed to return from Iraq for several months, so he figured he had plenty of time to learn how to walk.

"I wanted to walk when they came off the bus. [I wanted] to see all of them, but especially Doc," he said. "I wanted to shake his hand and say, 'Thank you.'"

In late December 2006, near the perfect rows of headstones that stretched up and along the hillsides at Arlington National Cemetery, the man in the wheelchair spoke in a soft, quiet southern drawl.

"To be honest," he said, "I'm pretty nervous about this."

"You'll do fine," his mother said.

The sergeant's body remained riddled with shrapnel wounds, pitting the skin on his entire left side with deep pink scars. What was left of his legs jutted from the wheelchair, filling only a fraction of his jeans, which were folded at the place where his knees used to be. Only one hand worked. He looked over at his wife and two daughters, at his parents, and at the rows and rows of white marble. Somewhere out there was a fresh grave.

As he entered for the first time the place known as our nation's most sacred shrine, the sergeant said he was unshaken by the seemingly endless headstones. What got to him, he said, were the people left behind.

"I just think about all the families and the people like myself who had to go into Arlington for this."

The sergeant's father wheeled him into a waiting room, where he asked to sit in the corner, out of the way. Soon the room was filled with crisp Navy uniforms—admirals, chiefs, and hospital corpsmen, many of them sporting dress coats that jingled with medals. Then down the stairs the sergeant saw the people who wore no uniforms, the ones who wore only grief. As it turned out, the man with no legs didn't need to learn how to walk. Doc's family walked over to him.

As Debra Anderson headed to the man in the wheelchair, she was immediately intercepted by another mother.

"Your son saved my son's life," Cheryl Edwards said through sobs, locking Debra in a hug. "I thank you. I thank you so much. And I'm sorry, so sorry."

The women embraced, and then the men did the same.

"He saved our son's life," Cheryl Edwards repeated.

Together the families walked to Sergeant Edwards, who sat with his three-year-old daughter, Paige, in his lap, and five-year-old Caitlin and his wife, Christina, by his side.

"I'm so glad you're here," Debra Anderson said.

"I wouldn't have missed it for the world," the sergeant said quietly. "I didn't give them a choice at the hospital. I told them I had to come."

"I know Christopher was so worried about you," Debra Anderson said. "He was so worried."

"He did everything right. Be proud of him," the sergeant said. "If it wasn't for him, I wouldn't be here. I wouldn't be able to hold my daughter on my lap."

Rick Anderson then bent down in a deep hug. With the knuckle of one finger he brushed the hand of one of the girls and smiled.

"Your boy kept me alive," Sergeant Edwards said. "I wanted to let go, and he kept me alive."

Kyle Anderson approached Edwards and during a long embrace told the Marine that he now carried part of his brother with him. Kyle told the sergeant he would always consider Sergeant Edwards his brother, too.

Then Sergeant Edwards looked up at Anderson's parents.

"If there's anything I can ever do for you, you let me know," he said.

"You just take care of these girls," Debra said, offering one of the largest smiles that many family members had seen since her son was killed. "We want to watch these girls grow up," she said.

From her father's lap, Paige pointed at Christopher Anderson's mother.

"Who dat?" the three-year-old asked.

"You'll understand one day, okay?" her grandmother said.

"Yes," the sergeant said, stroking her hair. "Daddy will tell you one day."

IN SECTION 60 of Arlington National Cemetery, the sun flashed off the bugle of a lone sailor who stood among the thousands of headstones. Dormant trees stretched toward the blue sky, holding blossoms that had turned brown.

As the Anderson family approached the casket and took their seats, six sailors surrounded it and lifted the flag.

The chaplain spoke and the rifle salute cracked. At the first few notes of taps, Sergeant Edwards hung his head and let his tears fall to his lap. The Navy honor guard folded the flag as if it were starched, slapping each fold into another. A rear admiral presented the flag to Debra. It was over in fifteen minutes.

Debra's sister, Sherry McDonald, took a bag filled with dark brown dirt collected from the home field of Doc Anderson's favorite baseball team, the San Diego Padres. Each family member took a fistful and dusted it on the casket. Debra placed her hand on the casket and held it there for several minutes. She let go slowly.

The sergeant's mother walked to Debra Anderson again, and they embraced.

"Greg says he wished it was him," she said, crying again. "He says he wishes that it was him who came home in the casket instead of Christopher."

The two women held each other for a long time.

"They all come home," Debra Anderson finally managed to say as they stood on the lime green artificial turf laid out over the mud where another family would soon stand. "They all come home."

AFTER EVERYONE ELSE climbed into their cars and prepared to leave, Rick Anderson stood with Kyle at the gravesite. The two men put their handprints in the dirt and smeared it on the casket. Kyle Anderson said he didn't want to leave his brother, and once again it fell to his father to persuade him to go.

For the past three weeks Rick Anderson had been the quiet rock, steadying his family, comforting them, looking out for everyone, the way he had taught his son. He spoke at his son's funeral in Colorado and said he cried long and hard during his private conversations with God. On the outside, with his friendly face and salt-and-pepper mustache, he looked more like the real estate broker that he is rather than a former member of one of the most elite special warfare units in the country.

But after all the quiet, all the stoicism, Rick Anderson stood at the empty gravesite, took a deep breath, and let out a Navy SEAL war cry that carried over the headstones.

"Hooyah, kid!" he shouted at his son's casket, his voice breaking. "You did good."

34

Marine Corporal
Brett Lee Lundstrom

Denver, Colorado

A T THE SUPERMARKET near the cemetery, the cashiers recognized the soft face of the Lakota woman.

"Every time I come down here, I buy eight bouquets—one for each of the Marines. Someone does it for Brett, so I do it for them," Doyla said as she gathered the flowers. "We all just kind of take care of each other's kiddos."

Although many relatives at the Pine Ridge reservation wanted Brett buried there, Doyla knew her son always wanted to go to Colorado. When the Marines pulled up at her home in South Dakota, she had already placed the house on the market. She moved to a Denver suburb after the funeral so that she could visit the cemetery at least once a week.

Inside the store, she turned to the red roses.

"I always bring Brett roses — a dozen red roses from me and a dozen from his brother even though he was never here."

That day for the first time Eddy was there. He appeared from a different aisle in the supermarket, carrying two cans of Budweiser.

"I want to have a beer with my brother," he said.

The day after Eddy arrived from Iraq, his mother lent him her cell phone to make a call. After speaking with a friend, he snapped the cell phone closed and saw her screen saver: his brother's headstone at Fort Logan.

"He slammed the phone down and walked off," she said. "He said, 'I can't see that right now.'"

During the wake for his brother at Pine Ridge, Eddy spent much of his time alone, in the bleachers of the gymnasium at Little Wound High School, dressed in his combat fatigues. According to the Department of Defense, any surviving sibling who has an immediate family member killed in action may request to be kept from further combat.

"At the wake, grandmothers were hugging him, crying, saying, 'Don't go,'" his mother said. "He said, 'I'm going to go back.' He said, 'I have a job to finish, and I can't leave my buddies behind.' Of course my thoughts were 'What about your mom?' But I didn't say anything. I would never have said don't go, because I know that would have made it hard on him. I said, 'Dad and I understand.'"

After he arrived back in the United States from his tour in Iraq and set out on a long road trip to clear his mind, Eddy saw an eagle from his car window.

"Mom," he told his mother later, "Brett was following me."

Inside Fort Logan National Cemetery, Doyla bent down and kissed her son's headstone. Then she laid out a picnic blanket.

Her niece placed the flowers on the graves of nearby Marines.

Eddy arrived and stood near his car for a few minutes before walking over. When the family first took him to the cemetery a month earlier, he refused to get out of the car. He eventually circled the grave but wouldn't look at it.

This time he approached the grave slowly, staring mostly at the clean gray back of the headstone.

Finally, he walked around, looked at his brother's name, and broke down.

The silence was shattered by the shots of a rifle salute from a nearby funeral. Moments later taps wafted through the cemetery.

Eddy drank half of his beer and poured the rest on his brother's grave.

Near Saddam Hussein's hometown of Tikrit, Eddy's tasks included cleaning up after the roadside bombs. He told friends about working his way through the carnage of twisted metal and twisted bodies.

"He's been through hell and back," his mother said. "Well, I don't know if he's back yet." She can't help thinking of his big brother's warning.

"Brett was really scared for Eddy. He said, 'The Army doesn't train them like the Marines. He's not ready.' He said, 'I'll be all right—I'll be home in three months. It's Eddy you need to worry about.'"

Two weeks earlier she had received a call in the middle of the night. After spending weeks trying to hold his emotions, Eddy called from his bunk at Fort Sill, Oklahoma, where he was alone, the first to return from leave.

"He said, 'Mom, I'm scared.' He was all alone, and it was hitting him all at once," she said. "He talked about the nightmares. He told me what he was thinking." He then described a place she recognized all too well.

"In the beginning, there was nothing, nothing that anybody could do for me. I wanted to die. Sometimes I think about it, and I still have those thoughts. That evil s-word"—suicide—"can creep into your thoughts," she said. "The pain was just so unbearable."

She heard the same worries in her son's voice, so she made a deal.

"I said, 'I know how you're feeling. You have to remember I hung in there for you, and you've gotta hang in there for me. You're the reason I'm still alive.'"

At the time, Eddy's new unit was scheduled to leave for Afghanistan in five months.

"My first instinct was to get him out," she said, "but if he wants to go, then all we can do is support him again."

Even though many in her own family argue against the Iraq war, she refused to take a stand, other than supporting her sons.

"I can't really blame anybody. Brett died doing what he wanted to do. He didn't want to die, but he was willing to die for us," she said. "He died doing what he was supposed to do. He died doing what they told him to do. That's what they do."

As Doyla packed up her things from South Dakota to move to Colorado, she found two coffee mugs she had planned to give her sons. Happiness is . . . "Iraq" in my rear-view mirror, the inscription reads. She still hasn't opened the boxes of Brett's belongings that were returned from Iraq. She had the Marines put them in the garage with the word deceased facing the wall.

According to Lakota tradition, she is supposed to burn all his belongings. She can't do it.

"I still sleep with his shirt," she said. "Not every night now, but I still sleep with it sometimes. I just hold it like a pillow. It makes me feel better."

Tradition says that Brett's spirit can hear her sobbing and feel her grief, which makes it more difficult for the spirit to make the journey to join his ancestors.

"Everyone keeps saying, 'Be strong. Don't cry,'" she said. "I guess you're supposed to be strong, but I'm not strong."

After she left the reservation, she followed Catholic traditions—both Eddy and Brett were altar servers—but she recently fell away from the church. A few months earlier at Pine Ridge she went through a healing ceremony that she said helped her work through her grief more than any other.

"It's being torn between the way we believe and the way I grew up, the way I lived my life all these years," she said. "I find myself praying to God and not Tunkashila, and that's where I still feel torn."

She stopped and sniffled.

"It's basically the same person," she said of the two deities.

In another month she was scheduled to have a ceremony at Pine Ridge—one that signals the end of the official mourning period.

"I guess that I'm supposed to go through a 'wiping of the tears' ceremony at a year," she said. "I won't be able to do it."

As a nearly full moon rose over the Badlands, a brilliant orange sunset stretched across Pine Ridge, setting aglow the tarp on the tiny sweat lodge. A bonfire had heated twenty-four rocks for several hours. Now it crackled as it slowly died. Before returning to the sweat lodge, Doyla's friends and relatives gathered, giving thanks to the "grandpas," the rocks that are reused for ceremonies. The grandpas, they say, were here before any of us and hold histories of their own. Still, the heat and water of the ceremony can crack them.

"In many ways the rocks are like people," Glorianna Cordova said earlier. "You can only use them a certain amount of times before they break."

They had planned to hold a Wopila, a ceremony in which Doyla would give thanks to the spirits for all the help they had given her through the process. Instead, she had to wait through her "sacred time," her menstrual cycle, when tradition holds that her body's own regenerative power would interfere with the power of the spirits in the sweat lodge. Still, her family decided to hold a sweat lodge without her—until she could return for her Wopila ceremony—and send their thoughts through the steam.

In the heat of the grandpas, the darkness enveloped them once again. They prayed for the ones left behind and those whose journey had just begun. For more than an hour they prayed and sang, hoping to lend strength to the woman who waited at the nearby motel.

Afterward, draped in a towel, sweat still coating his body, Marlin Under Baggage looked into what remained of the fire and thought of his nephew's spirit and his sister's tears.

"People mourn for themselves because they're left behind," he said. "If there is constant unhappiness, he hears that out there, and he wants to come back. It is supposed to be a joyous occasion, your birth and your death. Tonight will help us find that clarity, to work with it in a positive way."

Minutes later, once the sweat lodge had officially ended, the headlights of a car swept across the property. The woman with the soft face got out of her car and stood on the ground where she grew up, the land she still knows in the dark.

Doyla walked into the cold night, wrapped in the warmth of the coat embroidered with a lone eagle. She looked up at the shining fiery stars.

In the Lakota language, there is no word for good-bye.

35

Katherine, Jimmy, Caroline, and Jeff Cathey

Reno, Nevada

ORE THAN A year after James Cathey's death, his boyhood room in Reno still looks much the same as the day he left. His closet is filled with his clothes. A bookshelf near his camouflage-colored bedspread overflows with titles ranging from Western history to Greek philosophy.

Now, however, a makeshift shrine spills over his desk, including photos, dried flowers, a tin of Copenhagen, a shotgun shell, and an empty Knob Creek whiskey bottle.

Each time Katherine visits the home where her husband grew up in Reno, Nevada, she stays in his room, in his bed, and awakens to all that remains.

"I talk to some of my friends, and they say, 'Wouldn't that be rough, to be there in his room with all his stuff?'" Katherine said.

"You would think it would be rough, but it's not. I sleep better here than I've ever slept at home in Colorado. Maybe I feel like I'm with him when I'm here."

She sat cross-legged on his bed, holding a teddy bear.

"Sometimes I'll take one of his pictures and lie in bed next to it," she said. "I'll pick up one of the books he's read and read it. The hardest thing about being in here is that it makes it feel like he *is* here. Being around all his clothes and things, it's hard to separate that from him. But he's not here."

She heard a small voice just outside the room, and her face brightened.

"Hey there, Jimmy-doo," she said, cooing at the fourteen-month-old who waddled into the room.

Before her husband's death, Katherine had been in his parents' home only once and barely knew them. Since the baby's birth, she and her son have made several trips from their home in Colorado to Jim Cathey's hometown. More than eighteen months after his death, Katherine returned to Reno to accept additional honors that Jim would never see and learn of a new scholarship in his name.

As she watched the baby, she once again saw his father's smile.

"I swear that when he's in this room, Jimmy can see his dad," she said. "He stands in this corner, just standing there and talking. I wonder if he can see things that we can't—that kids, in general, can see things that we can't because we've programmed ourselves to be more skeptical."

She lifted him onto the camouflage blanket that camouflages nothing.

"Jimmy's always felt right at home here," she said, "like he had been here before."

C AROLINE CATHEY SAT in her bathrobe on the living room floor, gazing at the giant photo of her son on the wall. She then scooted over to the boy who carries his name.

"Where's dada? Where's dada?" she said, pointing the toddler toward the photo.

"Da-da-da," Jimmy said as his grandmother clapped.

The baby's presence transports Caroline and Jeff Cathey back to a time when another little Jimmy lived in the home. Caroline sings the songs she used to sing to her boy—the jingle from the old Frito Bandito commercial—and smoothes his skin with her fingertips, imitating the neck rubs she used to give her son. Jeff Cathey plays a soft head-butt game called "bonkers" with the boy and chases him around the house on hands and knees.

"He just brings that warmth back," Caroline said. Then she looked down at the boy and spoke in a baby voice.

"Could you stay here forever?" she said, cuddling him. "Could you stay here forever?"

Since their son's death, things have not moved on. The Catheys still go to work. They try to keep busy. Sometimes they succeed.

"I still have a huge hole in my heart, and sometimes you feel like you don't have enough tears," Jeff said. "A lot of times the tears are suppressed by medications, but you feel you need to cry.

Still, sometimes the tears flow. I don't know when it's going to happen."

Then it does.

"It's been more than a year," he said as he pulled out a handkerchief. "It's never going to be long enough ago."

When he is alone in his workshop, Jeff said, he still sometimes imagines the phone ringing.

"When I was at work, he used to just call up and say, 'Hey, Dad.' So sometimes I'll just pick up the phone at work and say, 'Hey, Dad.' It's his words coming out of my mouth. 'Hey, Dad.' But there's nobody there."

THE MARINES WERE at the door again. While Jim was overseas, the Catheys dreaded the dress blues visit. This time the mission was not nearly so somber as Major Beck and the other men in the sharp blue uniforms brought the medals that Jim Cathey's parents never received and began preparations for a ceremony in their home to present the honors properly.

Shortly after the Marines rang the doorbell, another woman arrived with a toddler. Theresa Tierney knew plenty about the Catheys and their struggles during the past eighteen months. It was her husband who told Jeff and Caroline Cathey that their son was dead. Although it pales in comparison to the Catheys' pain, she said, that day changed her family's life, too.

"That night [after the notification call], he was crying, quiet. I didn't know what to say," Theresa Tierney said of her husband, Winston Tierney, who had since been promoted to major. "He was quiet for a long time, and there was nothing I could do."

Eight months earlier Major Tierney was deployed to one of the most dangerous areas of Iraq. Now, Theresa Tierney says, she looks into the face of the war every time she sits down for tea with Caroline Cathey.

"It had a big impact on me. It's more of a reality of what can happen," she said and then stopped. "I can't talk much about it without crying."

She wiped the tears and then continued.

"Every time I turn the corner, I wonder if I'm going to see that Marine Corps van. Lying in bed, I'm always thinking, 'Am I going to get the knock?'"

As Theresa followed her two-year-old daughter into another room, she stopped to talk with the woman she hopes she never has to be.

"I want you to know that if there's ever anything I can do for you . . . anything," she told Katherine. "I mean that. If there's ever anything I can do. Anything."

The two women sat on the couch, watching the two toddlers.

"She's had a lot more problems than I thought," Theresa said, looking at her daughter. "She knows that Daddy's in Iraq. But one night I put her down to sleep, and she asked me if I was going to Iraq. I said, 'No, I'm going to the couch.' That's hard to hear from a two-year-old."

The two women sat quietly for a few minutes.

"People ask, 'How do you get through it?'" Theresa said, smiling. "And I say, 'firming eye cream.'"

"I use plenty of that, too," Katherine said.

In the room, Jeff Cathey—whom the little girl calls "Mr. Jeff"—chased the two-year-old on his fifty-one-year-old hands and knees, playing hide-and-seek.

"She thinks Mr. Jeff is Jimmy's dad," Theresa said.

A FEW FEET FROM James Cathey's boyhood bed, his parents constructed a field cross, just as the Marines had set up during their son's memorial service in Iraq.

When people ask her about having so many reminders in the house, Caroline shakes her head. The word *closure* sets her off.

"I've had people tell me to get over it," Caroline said. "I politely tell them, 'How about if I chop off your finger and see if it grows back?'"

She said she notices people avoiding her, still uncomfortable about speaking her son's name. At the grocery store, she said, some people will deliberately walk the other way, pretending not to recognize her.

"Just say hello," Caroline said. "Don't make me feel like I'm some kind of freak."

Katherine nodded.

"Everyone is really uncomfortable about it. How many people in their mid-twenties were widowed and left with a child?" she said. "My friends don't know how to broach the subject. I just don't think that anyone can attempt to comprehend what I'm going through."

Katherine has tried to restart her life, building a home and going back to work part-time in real estate. Meanwhile, she mainly keeps to herself, blocking out news of the war and concentrating on Jimmy and how to share him.

"I suppose I never could have come out here, never established a relationship with [Jim's parents]," Katherine said. "It's not easy to establish a relationship with your husband's family when you've never had one before. [But] being around Jim's family makes me feel like I'm with him. They make the same facial expressions. They have the same goofy stories and jokes."

Although Katherine and her husband differed in their views about the war—she was against the decision to invade Iraq, while he simply told her "I have a job to do"—she says their disagreements bonded them more tightly together.

Still, some days are more frustrating than others—especially the ones in which she sees another name crawl across the bottom of the television screen.

"It seems like they're just using our guys as guinea pigs," she said. "There are these IEDs all over Iraq, and they're sending our guys in to find them—to find them by getting blown up."

In his room the war widow and Gold Star mother looked at the stacks of condolences from politicians that still rest in a corner. The only condolence letter displayed is from the commandant of the Marine Corps.

"That's what meant the most to my son. He couldn't give a shit about the congressmen or the president. He cared for his men and the Marines," Caroline Cathey said. "The president, congressmen, they don't have any idea. They don't have any *clue* as to what you're feeling."

A s the Catheys gathered on the couch, Major Beck began a smaller version of his Remembering the Brave presentation, holding the medals that were never properly presented.

Ours is a dangerous life but for good reason. We need our own dangerous warriors to ensure that our freedoms are enduring. No one wants peace more than the fighting man, for they bear the weight and ultimate consequence of war more than anyone else.

The formally dressed Marine looked back at the medals, pausing dramatically as little Jimmy walked up beside him. The toddler bent over, with his head between his legs, and looked back at his family with a grin, adding a bit of levity that the family later said was trademark Jim Cathey.

Major Beck continued:

Time and time again we discover that our warriors who are in the arena serve one another first. And in doing so, they succeed in their higher missions. Jim . . . had a particular appreciation and love for

his Marines, and so he shared in their pain, their loss, and their dan-
ger. Ultimately, he cared less about himself than his Marines, which
is a mark of our finest leaders.

Major Beck presented medals to the Catheys and then brought out special Scholarship of Honor medallions from the Brian La Violette Foundation. He announced a special annual scholarship in Cathey's name, to be established at his high school in Reno.

After handing the medallions to the Catheys, Katherine, and Jim's sister, Joyce, he placed one set of medals aside for Jim Cathey's first child, Casey, who was born while Jim was in high school. Although the little girl and her family had not visited since the funeral, the Catheys said they hope that one day she will meet Jimmy and ask questions.

"I believe Casey is going to come to this home someday and want to know about her father," Major Beck said as he handed over the medals. "If that day comes, these are for her."

Major Beck then picked up Jimmy and placed the last medal around the little boy's neck. Major Beck had requested a special inscription for the back of Jimmy's medal: YOUR FATHER IS WATCH-ING OVER YOU.

AFTER THE CEREMONY had ended and the medals were tucked away, Caroline sat in the shadows of the living room, cradling her grandson as he fell asleep.

"How ya doing?" Jeff said, knowing the answer.

The little boy's grandmother smiled back as she ran her fingers through the toddler's wispy hair and along his downy skin.

"You wouldn't have it any other way, would you?" he said.

"No," she said.

Then they both realized what that meant.

"Well, I guess you would have it some other way," Jeff said.

She closed her eyes and continued to feather her fingertips across Jimmy Cathey's face.

"He's here," she said. "He's here, too."

36

Sam and Mary Holder, Jo, Bob, and Kris Burns

Fort Logan National Cemetery, Denver, Colorado

Sam and Mary Holder brought out a bouquet of flowers, a bucket, and a camera to Fort Logan National Cemetery.

"We have kind of a ritual. Mary cuts the flowers, and I make sure the water is there," Sam Holder Sr. said. "The last thing I do is take photos."

The ritual began more than a year before, when Jana Kramarova, their son's fiancée, sent twenty-seven red roses for what would have been his twenty-eighth birthday. Since she lived in Prague, Sam Holder Sr. took a photo of the flowers and sent it to her via e-mail. He did the same thing the next week and the next.

The photos capture the changing seasons. In October the flowers sprout from a pumpkin. In December snow covers the grave. In January artificial flowers contrast brown dormant grass.

The only constant is the dull, gray marble tombstone and its inscription.

Eventually, as families heard about Holder's photos, they asked if he could take pictures of their sons' graves, too. Soon Mr. Holder was e-mailing photos of Kyle Burns's grave to Kyle's parents in Laramie, and photos of Navy SEAL Danny Dietz's tombstone to his widow, Maria Dietz, who lives in Virginia; she calls the regular e-mails "a window to my husband's grave."

As they looked at the graves together in 2006, the couple realized that it would have been Kyle Burns's twenty-second birthday. Mary Holder placed flowers on the grave, and then, to their surprise, Kyle's mother and brother arrived at the cemetery after driving in from Laramie.

As the two families stood in the section of the cemetery that holds the casualties from Iraq and Afghanistan, they exchanged hugs.

"I didn't know it was Kyle's birthday today," Sam Holder Sr. said.

Jo Burns sniffled a yes.

"What are you going to be up to for the rest of the day?" Mary Holder said.

"Crying," Jo Burns said.

"I thought the hardest days would be the holidays, Christmas and Easter," she said. "But this is the hardest. Birthdays."

As they stood at the marker, they looked at the date they had in common, etched in stone.

"Veterans Day," said Kyle's brother, Kris.

As the afternoon wore on, only a few cars entered the cemetery. Before his son died, Sam Holder was one of those who had never been inside Fort Logan.

"You look at the war, and it only touches a few of us. It doesn't touch the majority of the American people," Sam Holder Sr. had said earlier. "What always bothered me was how disproportionately the whole war has affected people in the U.S."

He knelt down, propped his camera on another grave, and snapped photos of his son's grave. Then he walked to Danny Dietz's tombstone and took another picture.

The Holders said their son believed in the war and in what he was doing. His parents said they do, too. Despite their son's receiving the Silver Star, they don't dwell on the battle. They don't need to. In some ways, Sam Holder Sr. said, he has heard enough war stories. As a Vietnam veteran he has seen how too many of them end.

"I have friends whose names are on the Vietnam Memorial. You go there, and you think of how much life I've experienced that they never will."

When he got back to Kyle Burns's grave, he stopped.

"Sometimes I'll just stand back with the camera," he said as he looked at the grave, his wife, and Jo Burns. Sometimes, in addition to the gravestone photos, he said, he likes to capture the spontaneous moments that not enough people see, that not enough people want to see—those that continue long after the battle is over.

"Sometimes you can get some pretty touching pictures," he said.

At the foot of their sons' graves, the two mothers embraced once again. Sam Holder Sr. brought the camera to his face and pressed the button.

37

Major Steve Beck

Reno, Nevada

WHEN MAJOR BECK hands over the folded flag, he purposefully keeps his voice low.

"You know, everyone always wants to know what the words are, what it is that I say," he said during a long drive after another funeral. "I don't say it loud enough for everyone to hear."

There are scripted words written for the Marines to follow. As usual, Major Beck has his own.

"I'm basically looking into that mother, father, or spouse's eyes and letting them know that everyone cares about them," he said. "But the words are nothing compared to the flag."

He drove several miles without speaking. In his mind, the subject had not changed.

"You think about the field of cotton somewhere in Mississippi, and out of all of it comes this thread that becomes this flag that covers our brave. Think about it. I had a cotton field right behind the house when I was going to Air Command and Staff College. Imagine being that farmer who owned the cotton field. Imagine if one of those parents was able to take a flag back to him and say, 'That flag came out of your field and escorted my son home.'"

He shook his head.

"The things you think about," he said.

Usually on these long drives he steps back from it all, or at least he tries to. He still hasn't learned how to step back far enough.

"One morning after burying a lance corporal, all I wanted to do was come home and play with my children—just take them into a corner with all their things and play with them," he said. "But you know, all I was thinking about while I was playing with them were all those guys out there in harm's way, making all that possible. Here we are while they're out there. Someone could be under attack right now. Someone could be calling for an air strike . . ."

Someone could be standing at a door, preparing to knock.

"This experience has changed me in fundamental ways," Major Beck said. "I would not wish it on anyone, but at the same time I think it's important that it happened to me. I know it's going to have an impact on someone's life that I'm going to meet years from now. . . . It's like you've got them in inventory. You'll have them when you need them."

Over the years, he said, so many scenes return. The doors and doorbells. The first time he completed a final inspection. Sand on a casket. The scene he sees the most, however, is not of a single moment but the entire journey, viewed through someone else's eyes.

"One thing keeps coming back to me," he said. "It was during the memorial service for Kyle Burns."

The service came only a week after Major Beck first parked in front of that little white house in Laramie, watching the perfect snow, preparing to walk through it all. During that memorial service, Kyle Burns's uncle, George Elsom, recounted the call from his devastated sister who phoned him after she first saw the Marines at the door.

"At Kyle's memorial service, his uncle talked about all they had learned since that night," Major Beck said. "Then he looked at us and said something I'll never forget. He said, 'If these men ever come to your door, don't turn them away.' He said, 'If these men come to your door . . . let them in.'"

EPILOGUE

AUGUST 2007

It's not an ending. It's not a period at the end of their lives.
It's a semicolon. The story will continue to be told.

—STEVE BECK

Lieutenant Colonel
Steve Beck and
Sergeant Damon Cecil

L ONG AFTER MIDNIGHT in a hotel room, two Marines stood before a bronze eagle sculpture and draped it with dog tags, trying to figure out what it all meant.

"You can think of a million different things behind this," said the man whose white gloves had touched so many families. "I think everyone's going to have a separate meaning in their own mind. That's the magic in doing this. They're all going to see something different."

Two months earlier, Steve Beck had been promoted to lieutenant colonel after being transferred from Colorado to Washington, D.C., to work on a crucial air defense program. He returned to Denver to receive his promotion in a ceremony in which he asked his wife and children to pin the oak leaf on one shoulder. For the other shoulder he had invited a group of women whom he also calls his family: a group of Gold Star mothers.

He returned to Colorado again in the summer of 2007 to hold the largest Remembering the Brave ceremony he had ever undertaken: thirty-nine fallen service members—not just Marines this time but soldiers, sailors, and airmen who did not receive their medals in what he considered a proper setting.

In the room he looked at the bronze eagle. Like the man, the eagle is both hard and soft. Its talons and beak are bared, but the ferocity is carried on feathers.

"For me it's biblical," Beck said. "There's the line, 'They will soar on wings like eagles.'"

The other Marine, Sergeant Damon Cecil, also eyed the eagle as he draped another dog tag on a feather.

"I don't see it as biblical. I see the eagle as our country and the dog tags being the dead, but the dead are part of the feathers. With the dog tags on it, the country is carrying our dead, but if the dead aren't there, our country can't fly."

The newly commissioned lieutenant colonel looked at him, impressed.

"I don't know," Sergeant Cecil said, shrugging. "I'm just a Marine."

Sergeant Cecil had actually attended more funerals than Steve Beck. He had served in the honor guard since the beginning of the war, carrying the first Coloradans brought home and then more than a dozen after that. Unlike his superior officer, he had seen the war from both sides. Before he went to Iraq, however, Damon Cecil never spoke to the dead.

"When you're carrying them home without going over there, you have this respect, but it's a respect you don't understand," he said. "When you go over there and come back, you say, 'Man, now not only do I understand, but I want to talk to them.' I feel like I know them. I feel like I'm going to walk with him all the way to the grave."

Only a few weeks before the ceremony, he returned to Colorado for another funeral. When the private jet arrived, Sergeant Cecil was one of the first Marines in the belly of the plane to remove the casket.

"When I got up in there, I talked to him. I said, 'Hi, brother,' and smoothed the cardboard before taking it off," he said. "I talk to them all the time. I say, 'I'm here for you, brother. I'm here to take you home.'"

It's a one-way conversation that continues as he posts guard near the casket.

"I come into the room, and I post right next to him. I say, 'Hey, brother, I'm going to take care of you for a while. I'll be here for a while and then another Marine will take over.'"

He stopped. "Maybe that sounds weird. I'm not the type of guy who's going to go and talk to a casket. But now I do it without even thinking about it."

Sergeant Cecil's grandfather fought in Normandy. His father was in Vietnam. Less than a week after returning from Iraq—still shaking off the sand—he volunteered to help then–Major Beck with the first Remembering the Brave ceremony. Although he was later stationed in California, he returned for the next two. Like Lieutenant Colonel Beck, he says he has no choice. He was there for the first funerals when the streets of Denver were lined with supporters. He has also served at the recent funerals when those in attendance are composed primarily of family and friends.

"I feel like the world has changed the channel," he said. "When the soldiers started dying at the beginning, it was like this big movie on the screen. And now it's like it's gone to DVD. It's on the shelf. . . . Those yellow stickers, it was like they were cool for a while, but everything seems to come as a fad, a big wave. But the wave crashes."

The two men worked for a while in silence, until they had hung the last of the dog tags. By then they had been awake for nearly two days straight trying to organize the ceremony.

Lieutenant Colonel Beck picked up the eagle and carried it to a desk, and the tin tags clinked.

"They sound almost like wind chimes," Sergeant Cecil said.

"It's the sound of freedom," said Lieutenant Colonel Beck.

Melissa Givens

ONE DAY BEFORE the ceremony, Melissa Givens sat in the Department of Motor Vehicles office, alongside a man in camouflage who was not her husband, waiting for a reminder she had to pay for.

"Did you call in about this license plate?" the woman asked.

"I called in," Melissa said. "It's a Fallen Soldier plate."

"Oh," said the woman. "I've never done one of those before. This is my first time putting one in."

"You're the first again, Melissa," said Lieutenant Colonel Sprague Taveau, who had accompanied Melissa to the office.

"We're always the first," said the widow of the first Fort Carson soldier to die.

As the woman left to get the plates, Melissa sat back in her chair.

"The plates actually cost twenty-five dollars extra, which is pretty shitty," she said. "Actually, it's very shitty."

It is one of many frustrations she has had to face as one of the first widows of the war. It took her nearly a year to receive her husband's Purple Heart because the Army initially classified Jesse's death as an accident. She has had problems with the boys' health insurance. She still has to fill out forms proving the children are not married in order to receive benefits. In this military town, widows still don't receive special treatment in such places as the hospital and the DMV, where uniformed soldiers have their own special line.

"You always have to have someone in uniform with you to go to the front of the line. I don't have him anymore," Melissa said. "What do they want me to do? Bring in his empty uniform? Do they want me to bring in the urn with his ashes?"

To make sure she didn't have to wait, Sprague took his lunch break to bring her to the DMV in his uniform. The lieutenant colonel was pulled back from Iraq after his wife was diagnosed with terminal cancer; she died several months after he returned from the war. Eventually, he found a friendship with Melissa, and they started dating.

"I guess I'm your E-CAO," he said, "your extended casualty assistance officer."

She had not heard from her original CAO for more than a year. She was never assigned someone to take his place.

"Last I heard, he was in Baghdad," she said.

The license plate lady returned and began typing.

"Are you active duty?" the woman asked Melissa.

"My husband *was*," she said, raising an eyebrow.

The woman paused and then held up her hand.

"No need to say anything else," she said, finally making the connection. "I'm so sorry. I don't really know what to say. I guess nobody ever really knows what to say."

Melissa said nothing. The woman continued to type, doing her best at small talk, and finally handed over the license plate.

On the way home they talked about the latest poll numbers that showed declining support for the war—which, despite all her frustrations, she still supported. She has asked that Jesse's name be taken off peace protests that include the names of the dead, such as the empty boots project that toured the nation.

"I went to one of the Web sites, and someone had written, 'How many people do you have to kill for college money?' That kind of stuff. That's the kind of people they are. I know there's freedom of speech, but you can intentionally hurt people with your freedom of speech. The war sucks, but as a country we made a decision to go in there, and we have to support them," she said. "We have to support what they're doing."

She follows the news but doesn't think much of politicians. She still can't believe all the red tape that widows must endure long after their husbands are gone. When she met with President Bush after her husband's death, she said she was appreciative of the gesture but was not awestruck.

"He's just a man," she said. "He's not my husband."

When she types messages on the computer these days at fallen heroesmemorial.com, her messages are more upbeat. She has begun to volunteer with the group that initially helped her, including the Tragedy Assistance Program for Survivors. With the help of everyone who has sent condolence cards and posted online messages of support, she says, she gets closer to moving on, while still remembering.

It means so much to us when we log on here and see that he is still touching people. Your words are very comforting to us in our crazy lives. After almost four years the pain at times is still unbearable. Time does not heal all wounds. Keeping his memory alive is one of the most important things I will do in my life, not only for my children and myself, but for everyone who sometimes forget what our freedom cost. So again thank you to all that help me with this by taking the time to write your thoughts and feelings on this site. Your words do ring out to us. We do read and reread every post. All of you have made a difference to us.

After returning from the DMV and parking the car in Melissa's garage, Sprague closed the sun visor where she still keeps a photo of Jesse next to all her compact discs. Sprague has done all he can to get close to Melissa, asking her to marry him and giving her an engagement ring, but she is still not ready. Jesse's picture still hangs on every wall of her home. Sprague bought the home next door, which she says has worked out well. It takes time.

"It doesn't bother me," he says of the shrines to her husband. "It bothers a lot of people who come into her home, but not me. Every little thing I do pales in comparison to the sacrifice that Jesse made. I never knew Jesse, but I've had friends of my own who've died over there."

While Dakota and Carson played in the driveway, Sprague screwed in the Fallen Soldier license plate.

"I don't try to compete with him. I understand the love that was there—that is there still. I can't win that fight. She still loves him, and I understand that," he said. "Quite frankly, I see him as a brother in arms."

He finished tightening the screws and looked at the plate. "I never knew him," he said, "but I know him through the people I love."

Dakota and Carson Givens

DAKOTA GIVENS SAT on a bench at the neighborhood playground, watching the little boy who looks like the man he barely got to know.

"Sometimes I think Daddy is with Carson," Dakota said. "He looks just like him."

They still fight like brothers, wrestling and bopping each other on the head, and after a while Dakota will say, "I wish my brother got along with me," and then a few minutes later he is kissing the kid on the cheek and Carson is offering up another rivalry-melting "I wuv you, Kota."

At times Dakota remains confused and frustrated about his dad. Sometimes he will use it as an excuse to con his mother into giving in. Sometimes, he said, it all boils over. In early 2007 the nine-year-old tried to run away from home. He went about three blocks before Sprague caught up with him, and his mother grounded him for three months.

The frustrations come from everywhere, he said. The worst is the teasing.

"I get mad when kids tell me the wrong things, like 'Your daddy died for no reason.' They tell that to me. They even tell that to Carson. Kids are—well, kids are just kids. I know it's not true. And I make sure Carson knows that, too."

It is a kind of protection that most ten-year-olds don't need when looking out for their kid brother. Melissa still worries that he has grown up too fast. He is the closest person to an adult she has in the home, and she knows she sometimes treats him that way: the man of the house.

"If I get sad, I don't cry," Dakota said. "I cry in my mind, because when I cry, I get laughed at. So I cry in my mind."

They played on the slides and monkey bars until they were both red-faced. Then they headed home past the houses where the other soldiers still live.

"Careful, Carson!" Dakota said, stopping the four-year-old before he got too close to the street.

He took his brother's hand and looked both ways.

Rick, Debra, and
Kyle Anderson

D EBRA ANDERSON KEEPS several cardboard boxes
filled with more than six hundred letters received
from across the country. One of the boxes means
more than the others.

"These are from all the people who have lost children," she
said as she lifted letters from the box. "I didn't realize there would
be so many."

She picked up a letter from a man whose son died while on
active duty in 2001—a letter handed to her by a grief-stricken man
inside Arlington National Cemetery on the same day the Andersons buried their son.

"His face—It looked like his son had died yesterday," Debra

Anderson said. "I looked at Rick, and I thought, 'Are we going to hurt this bad five years from now?'"

She looked back toward the letters. "I've been around the Navy all my life and thought I knew everything about it," she said. "I know how to be a Navy wife. I know how to be a Navy mom. So many in my family were in the Navy. But no one has ever not come home. I never had any training on how to be the mother of a boy who wasn't coming home."

Near the letters are copies of condolences from military officials, and one from the president.

"I personally have a great respect and love for President Bush," Debra Anderson said. "I'm sure it has been very hard for him to personally sign three thousand condolence letters."

Despite her loss, she said, she tries not to think about the politics of the war.

"I don't have enough information to know if the war is right. One time on the phone I asked Christopher, 'Is this war worth it?' And he said, 'I don't know about the war, but I do know that these people need us here because they can't protect themselves.'"

During his phone calls home, Christopher rarely talked of the danger. Instead, he talked about the Iraqi people who lived through it every day.

"Christopher said, 'They're just regular people,'" his mother said. "'It's just like Frontier Street, except so beat up. There are husbands and wives and kids just trying to make it.'"

The military presence in Iraq continues to reshape the family.

After years of living his life in the moment, Kyle Anderson remembered a conversation/argument with his brother when Christopher told him to quit the delivery job and find work that would give his life a sense of meaning. Since his brother's death, Kyle—with the financial support of his parents—has dedicated his time to organizations that help veterans.

"It gives me a chance to live in honor of my brother," Kyle said. "Instead of going to some mundane job where I'm always thinking about my brother, I can go to a job and live for my brother."

The week before the Andersons left to attend the Remembering the Brave ceremony, they received a call from Navy Corpsman John Dragneff, who had escorted Doc Anderson's body home to Longmont. Dragneff was on his way to Iraq.

As she continued to sift through the letters, Debra Anderson shook her head. "They all call him a hero, a hero," she said. "As a mother I see my son in a lot of ways, but I gotta say I still can't grasp that word."

Her son learned to embrace the word but not for himself. One week before his death, he wrote his family a rare letter.

"*What up old man—I mean, Chief,*" Rick Anderson read from the beginning of the letter. He then lost his smile. "*This place is as bad as you can imagine, and the devil has his throne across the street from me.*"

The family wrote Christopher frequently, but he never wrote back, preferring to call. As they read the letter, they surmised why it was never sent.

"He didn't want you to worry," Kyle said as he got to the section of the letter where his brother wrote of losing a good friend in combat. Then, wide-eyed, he read the prophetic words that followed: *"It is hard on me and the guys, but I could only imagine what his family is thinking. He was a great kid and him and I joked around all the time. He will be missed here. A thing like this is why we think about life, love, and happiness in a new light. For me, writing about it is my way of letting him go and embracing my memories and trying to rid the fear. He died with a great fight and love for us and his country. He will never be forgotten. He is a true hero and Marine."*

Doc Anderson's Marines

THE 1-1 MISFITS looked at the empty uniform in the hallway of the hotel and straightened the shoulder bearing the caduceus. Every squad has a nickname. Doc Anderson fit in with the misfits.

"We called ourselves misfits because we were like the orphan children, and Sergeant Ed was our dad," said Lance Corporal Douglas Cianchetta. "Andy was our doc."

They have all visited with Sergeant Edwards, who continued to beat all expectations for recovery but couldn't make it to the ceremony in Denver.

"I believe Andy was put here to save Sergeant Ed's life," said Corporal Clinton Fort. "He was all about what I call 'doing the do.' He would do it."

As they stood in the place called the Hall of Heroes, where uniforms that will never be worn again were set up on the torsos of mannequins, they talked about Doc Anderson's nicknames: Supersailor and Devilsquid. "That boy was ninenty-nine percent Marine and one percent sailor," said Lance Corporal Cianchetta, who had Anderson's name, Doc Andy, tattooed on his shoulder.

In front of their doc's empty uniform, the misfits conjured images from Iraq, of Doc playing soccer with the kids, always trying to get his picture taken. After he patched up the leg of an Iraqi girl, the squad says, he had a friend for life. That turned out to be only a few months.

"When we told her mother what happened, she bawled," Corporal Fort said. "She wrote his name in Arabic and put it on her wall. She said, 'He's family.' He always wanted to make a change, and he did for at least one family in Iraq."

The misfits gathered around the empty uniform.

"All of us came back because of him," Corporal Fort said. "We all made it—all because of Doc."

Jo Burns and Mary Holder

T THE FIRST Remembering the Brave ceremony, Jo Burns confronted Steve Beck after she received her son's medals.

"I told him he could take his damn medals and . . . humph," she said, using a universal gesture to show him where he could stick them. "I told him I wanted my son back."

She paused.

"He set me straight. He said that the medals weren't for me, they were for Kyle."

Although the Marines in Kyle's unit did not return for the ceremony, some of them still visit Wyoming to hunt and hike with the Burns family. The vast majority of the Marines in Red Platoon have left the military.

"After the whole incident in Najaf and Fallujah, I was done," said former Lance Corporal Mike Ball, speaking on the phone from his home in Texas. "I don't think I was ready to lose any more friends again."

Many of them spent the past year in the open grassland, ranching together. One went to Bible college.

"I've got a framed picture of Kyle in my room," Lance Corporal Ball said. "Pretty much every time I look at my Purple Heart, my Navy Commendation Medal . . . I think of him, and I think I wasn't worthy to get those because Kyle died getting his. All I have is some shrapnel in my eye and my leg. Anytime there's a lull or a break, there's Kyle, there's Sam. . . . They're the epitome of what a friend should be. They brought my friends back."

In the hospitality room at the hotel, Jo Burns spotted Mary Holder and, just as she had on the day their sons were buried, walked into her embrace.

"That first hug [at the cemetery], it was such a shallow, empty time, but at the same time to know that there was someone else who had that same loss," Jo said. "It wasn't a satisfying hug. It was just a hug of 'I'm so sorry, because I know how you feel.'"

This time the hug held something else.

"Now when I hug Mary, when I hug Sam, I feel we've been through the same thing," she said. "They're hugs of friendship."

Katherine, Jimmy, and
Caroline Cathey

THE BOY WITH her son's name scurried across the room, and then Caroline Cathey scooped him into her arms.

"Oh, I love these hugs. I'm in heaven," she said to Jimmy Cathey. "You my heaven man. Where you been all my life? Where?"

Caroline and Jim's sister, Joyce, had spent the day at a seminar organized by the Tragedy Assistance Program for Survivors, which brings together the families left behind and holds daylong grief camps for the children.

As much energy as they drew from little Jimmy, they remained emotionally drained.

"All this is kind of a mixed bag," Caroline said. "It draws up all those old feelings, but also it lets you know they still care. It's like you save up all these emotions and you hold them in, and here you can let them out. . . . After these things, you feel like someone's poured sand in your eyes. But you do feel better. You do."

On the bed in her hotel room, Katherine Cathey nodded.

"I was telling my counselor that a lot of times when I start getting emotional, I try to change my thoughts so I can pull myself back together because if I fell apart, how can I take care of Jimmy? And maybe because I hold so much of it in, it's harder for me to come to these things," she said. "I never forget about Jim. It's not like I forget about him, it's just that . . . it brings the funeral emotions back."

Caroline once again cradled the little boy in her arms as Jimmy Cathey reached out for his father's medals.

Doyla Lundstrom

O N THE DAY that would have been Brett Lundstrom's twenty-fourth birthday, Doyla Lundstrom was alone. She knew her roots lay deep in the Black Hills, but her son was buried in Denver, where he said he wanted to be. She sat at his grave that day for hours. She still couldn't bring herself to wipe the tears. She went home and typed a letter that she sent to everyone on her e-mail list.

My name is Doyla Lundstrom and I lost my oldest son in Fallujah, Iraq, on Jan. 7, 2006. I have not been the same since. Luckily, my youngest son, who is in the Army, Spc. Edward Lundstrom Jr., made it home after serving a year there. Both of my sons deployed within 18 days of each other. My Marine, Brett, on Sept. 18, 2005, and my soldier, Edward, on Oct. 6, 2005. One hundred eleven days into Brett's deployment, his life was cut short by a sniper's bullet to the back of his neck. He never stood a chance. He knew he wasn't coming home, but he went anyway, because he had to. June 12 would have been his 24th birthday. The pain of losing a child is excruciating. Not a moment goes by that I am not thinking of my son. He was a beautiful child. I want the president to know that I am very upset that this war is still going on and we are losing more of our babies every day. Every time I hear on the news that more of our kids were killed, I feel the same pain for another mother somewhere. I wish he could feel the pain we do. Every day when I would come home from work and there wasn't a government vehicle parked in front of my house, I was ecstatic. That meant both of my babies were fine. On Jan. 7, 2006, I wasn't home when they did come to my door. It was a good thing that I wasn't. I am left with one son now who is still serving his country. He went back to war in Tikrit after taking two weeks of emergency leave. He did what he wanted to, and so did my oldest son, but that doesn't keep the pain away. I am very proud of my two sons; they are my heroes. Ask the president to bring our boys and girls home now.

"I didn't think about the big picture in the beginning," she said. "Maybe I was just in shock. Maybe it's just because I knew how Brett felt. He wanted to be doing what he was doing. He wanted to be in Iraq. . . . I don't know. I just don't know."

Doyla has since moved back to the Pine Ridge reservation in South Dakota to be near the land she can see in the dark, the place the military lifestyle kept her from for so long. In a way her son's death has helped her realize who she is and always has been. She is attending more sweat lodges and powwows and is learning about the traditions that she says bond her even closer to her son.

Still, she keeps in touch with Brett's buddies, many of whom came to the Remembering the Brave ceremony, most of them in civilian clothes. They came for Brett, they said. They came even more for the woman they call Ma.

"Yeah, this is Ma," said one of the Marines. "Lord knows I see her more than I see my own ma."

At the table they told drunken stories of the nights spent at Doyla's home in Virginia, blowing off steam, knowing they would leave for Camp Lejeune with a hug. When the Marines in Brett's unit returned from Iraq, they were met by Doyla, and, to their surprise, the hugs were still there.

The first night they met, a Marine named Joshua Frazier showed Doyla a tattoo on his thigh. At the top of the tattoo were two words: THE PRICE. Underneath was listed all the names of the Marines he had lost in battle. Brett's name was the second from the bottom.

After they returned home, nearly all the Marines in Brett's squad refused to reenlist. Josh had already made up his mind.

"He said, 'I'm going back for your son,'" Doyla said. "I said, 'Don't do it, because if anything happens, I know how your mom will feel.'"

He carried the tattoo back to Iraq and was killed a few months later. His name is now tattooed on someone else's arm.

Betty Welke

WAS IT WORTH it?

The question had echoed in Betty Welke's mind since she posed it to the major in her living room in Rapid City on the day that would have been Joe's twenty-first birthday. At the time, Major Beck had told her he couldn't answer that question for her; she had to decide it for herself.

"I've answered that question now," she said. "No, it wasn't worth it. I'm speaking for myself here," she said. "I don't know how Joe felt. He said, 'It's my job,' and left it at that."

She feels that her Joe died because medical care was stationed too far from her son during the battle of Fallujah. When she talks, she speaks softly, so none of the other families can hear her anger.

"The public doesn't want to deal with it because heaven forbid they were wrong. Heaven forbid they take responsibility for all these deaths. They were the ones who went to the polls," she said. "Yes, there are guys that are doing good over there. But are we doing it for our country or theirs? I think we made a mistake because we didn't understand the culture. We made a mistake."

Still, despite those feelings, she remains amazed by the comfort she found in the arms of Major Beck and his Marines after her son's death. Remembering the Brave—all the pomp and formality, all the flag-waving and tears—was transformed into an annual event at her urging.

"I had heard stories of how other families were treated, and I knew that each of these guys deserved the same recognition that Joe got," she said. "They deserve it. It's the least they deserve."

Remembering the Brave

Lieutenant Colonel Beck picked up the bronze eagle, left his hotel room, and headed downstairs to meet the empty platoon.

Thirty-nine uniforms lined the hallway, surrounded by family photos of the service members with their families, their awards, and their citations. Family members stood near the busts and tried to smile for the camera. Some of them wept instead.

Beck eventually wants to hold ceremonies in every state or maybe just a massive one in Washington, D.C.

"It's not just the Marines and the family who need to see it," he said earlier. "Society needs to see it. Over and over and over. Because we need to remember. This nation's at war, and we're all a part of it, and we need to share it."

Before a previous ceremony he said that the medals no one will ever wear should be the ones that reflect the most.

"It's not an ending. It's not a period at the end of their lives. It's a semicolon," he said. "The story will continue to be told."

As he started the ceremony, the ballroom once again fell silent. He read the citations one by one as the troops brought out the medals along with the vases of yellow roses.

By the time the room finally emptied it was after midnight. Still, nearly every family walked up to look at the bronze eagle onstage that the two Marines had spent so much time assembling—the symbol with a different meaning for everyone in the room.

Kyle Burns's uncle ran the back of a finger through the dog tags and listened as the names chimed together.

Author's Note

THERE ARE NOT enough names in this book.

When I interview a family who has lost a loved one in the war, I promise them to keep their name in print at every chance. In many ways, that's all they ask. Their names—and the names of their family members left behind—should always come first:

Marine Lance Corporal Thomas Slocum, Army Private First Class Jesse Givens, Army Staff Sergeant William Latham, Army Sergeant First Class Daniel Aaron Romero, Army Chief Warrant Officer Hans Gukeisen, Army Staff Sergeant Michael B. Quinn, Army Sergeant Keman Lavor Mitchell, Army Staff Sergeant Mark Lawton, Marine Sergeant Douglas Bascom, Marine Lance Corporal Andrew Riedel, Army Specialist Brian H. Penisten, Marine Lance Corporal Kyle Burns, Marine Staff Sergeant Theodore Sam Holder II, Marine Lance Corporal Greg Rund, Army Private First Class Robert W. Murray Jr., Army Specialist Ricky W.

Rockholt Jr., Army Specialist Travis W. Anderson, Marine Lance Corporal David Abeyta, Senior Airman Kristopher Mansfield, Army Private First Class Henry Risner, Marine Second Lieutenant James J. Cathey, Marine Corporal Brett Lee Lundstrom, Army Staff Sergeant Justin Vasquez, Army Private First Class George Geer, Army Captain Russell Brian Rippetoe, Army Sergeant Thomas F. Broomhead, Marine Lance Corporal Chance R. Phelps, Army Private First Class Tyler R. MacKenzie, Army Sergeant First Class Randall Scott Rehn, Marine Lance Corporal Chad Maynard, Army Staff Sergeant Michael C. Parrott, Army Sergeant Derrick Lutters, Navy Gunner's Mate Second Class Danny Dietz, Marine Lance Corporal Andrew Patten, Marine Sergeant Joshua J. Frazier, Marine Lance Corporal Justin Ellsworth, and Navy Hospital Corpsman HM3 Christopher Anderson.

Now there are too many names in this book.

I FIRST MET Major Steve Beck among the graves.

During the previous two years, Fort Logan National Cemetery had become part of my regular workplace. By 2004, I knew many of the cemetery workers by name, and they knew me—"our little Harry Potter," one of them called me, owing to my glasses and too-young-to-be-doing-this face. I had attended nearly a dozen military funerals since the start of the war, following the bodies until the last shovel of dirt fell on the graves. I had sat in countless living rooms, flipping through scrapbooks, trying to tell the stories of men and women I had never met. I sat on the floor and played with children who would never see their fathers. I listened to widows read their husband's last words. In a small northwestern Colorado town, I watched as a little boy the same age as my son ripped the rose boutonniere off his grandfather's lapel and placed it in the casket with his father's body.

It was nearly as difficult to watch a different sort of good-bye, as troops left on deployment. I'll never forget the Army medic who stood in a gymnasium before sunrise with his daughter dressed as a princess—complete with flouncy pink dress—and his son dressed in a replica of his own desert camouflage. That boy would later spend the night outside his home with his mother, eating military rations and camping, pretending he was with his dad in the desert. I stood in a bedroom, hours before another soldier deployed, watching as a woman placed seductive pictures of herself inside her husband's Bible. I entered a delivery room minutes after a baby was born to a woman who reached out for a hand that was not there. I listened as a teenage girl told me how she was sent to the principal's office for taking her lipstick and writing on her school's bathroom mirror, *What do you do when your* Mom's *in Iraq?*

Inside Fort Logan National Cemetery, I told Major Beck I wanted to follow him, to learn the resonance of the knock. I shared with him some of the scenes I had witnessed while covering the war at home. He had seen many of the same scenes, and he agreed the full story had not yet been told. The reason it had not been told, he said, was that it couldn't be told.

Before Major Beck gave access to the families he called his own, he required that we first get their approval. With very few exceptions, they welcomed us. They wanted to tell the stories of their sons. They wanted to make sure that people remembered.

Throughout those first weeks with Major Beck, he grilled me and photographer Todd Heisler, trying to detect any hidden agenda. Our goal was never political, I told him. All I wanted to do was write down what I saw.

Finally, before agreeing, he told us we had to be ready for a long journey. Then he told us we had to be ready to, in his words, "make it real."

Make it real? I thought. *How much more real could it get?*

I had no idea.

THE SCENES IN this book are true. I witnessed most of them firsthand, and have the tear-smeared notebook to prove it. The scenes that have been reconstructed—primarily the actual casualty notifications—are reported after research and verification from eyewitnesses.

For most of those scenes, I was accompanied by amazing photographers from the *Rocky Mountain News,* who also have my endless thanks. I only hope the words live up to the images.

Without Todd Heisler, many of the most stunning photos—as well as the words that accompany them—wouldn't exist. From freezing-cold nights in South Dakota to late night/early morning cathartic conversations in Reno, he was always there. We fed off each other's commitment, listening and looking together. Reporters can learn a lot from photographers. Everyone can learn something from Todd.

I never set foot in Iraq—my assignment was always this home front— but I imagine the same book could be written from the viewpoint of the Iraqi families who live every day on the actual front line. Until that book is written, this one is for them, too.

WHEN I FIRST met Major Beck, I wasn't sure how we would get along. I knew little of the culture of the Marines—I had spent time with the families of the fallen, but knew little of the men who carried the caskets for the last time. I had never served in the military, and was only beginning to learn the acronym-studded jargon.

An editor at the newspaper pointed out a crucial similarity she said she saw in both Beck and myself. "You have caring in common," she said.

It was a similarity I've seen reflected in so many places since: the entire caretaking crew at Fort Logan National Cemetery, the rumbling power of the Patriot Riders, and the grizzled faces of the All-Volunteer Honor Guard. Then there were the amazing people at the Pine Ridge Indian Reservation, whose traditions of honor and remembrance hold lessons for us all.

None of these stories would have seen print without the support of the *Rocky Mountain News*. Before we completed the newspaper version of "Final Salute," publisher John Temple called the staff into a room. "There's a point in this story where Sheeler talks about the Marines folding the flag for the last time," he said. "I want each of you to take the same care with this story. That's how much it means to me."

I am ultimately grateful for his guidance and permission to use the words and photos that his dedication made possible. Also at the *Rocky*, Jim Trotter and Mike Littwin helped me find the soul of the story, and a fleet of reporters and editors helped tune it—among them: Chris Barge, Kevin Vaughan, David Montero, John Moore, Tim Burroughs, Sonia Doctorian, Steve Miller, Tonia Twichell, Cliff Foster, Steven R. Nickerson, Judy DeHaas, Janet Reeves, Dean Krakel, Lynn Bartels, and Tina Griego.

Thanks to Dan Conaway for contacting me in person to talk about a very personal book at a very dark time, and for Simon Lipskar at Writer's House for lighting the way. At Penguin Press, Jane Fleming was instrumental in helping me realize this was all one story, and Ann Godoff allowed me to share it.

AUTHOR'S NOTE

The eyes of countless readers helped shape the book, among them two of the professors who showed me how to mix journalism and story-telling, Garrett Ray and John Calderazzo. Also, thanks to the eyes of Brady Dennis, John Diedrich, Maria Carrillo, Wright Thompson, Reid Forgrave, Gwen Florio, Ellen K. Graham, and Matt Tullis. Special thanks to the story saviors of gangrey.com, especially Ben Montgomery, whose encouragement after reading the first words was inspiring, and Thomas Lake, who spent countless hours picking over every last word.

Also thanks to Jack Jackson for helping to mold the story from far away, and to Pat Riley, Allen Bean, Kenneth Held, and John Aden for, in many ways, helping to mold me.

My grandfather served in Europe during World War II but rarely shared his stories. This book is also a nod to him, and to the compassion passed down from my parents, Jim and Sue Sheeler, and my sisters, Cassie and Amy.

Most importantly, my wife, Annick, and son, James, made it possible to step away from the emotion and into their arms. Their hugs are medicine.

But there are still not enough names in this book.

For each of the service members listed, there are thousands more names of people who have helped them and helped me. Their courage and encouragement is woven into every line. My words will never equal their deeds.

A PORTION OF THE PROCEEDS OF THIS BOOK WILL BE DONATED TO CHARITIES SUPPORTING MILITARY FAMILIES.